If Aristotle's Kid
Had an iPod

If Aristotle's Kid
Had an iPod

ANCIENT WISDOM FOR MODERN PARENTS

CONOR GALLAGHER

SAINT BENEDICT + PRESS

Charlotte, North Carolina

Cover design by Chris Pelicano.

Library of Congress Cataloging-in-Publication Data
Gallagher, Conor.
   If Aristotle's kid had an iPod : ancient wisdom for modern parents / by Conor Gallagher.
      p. cm.
   Includes bibliographical references (p. 205).
   ISBN 978-1-61890-414-0
1. Aristotle. Nicomachean ethics. 2. Ethics—Study and teaching. 3. Parenting—Religious aspects—Christianity. 4. Child rearing—Religious aspects—Christianity. I. Title.
B430.G35 2012
171'.3—dc23   2012027437

Published in the United States by
Saint Benedict Press, LLC
PO Box 410487
Charlotte, NC 28241
www.saintbenedictpress.com

Printed and bound in the United States of America.

"You know that the beginning is the most important part of any work, especially in the case of a young and tender thing . . ."
—Plato (Aristotle's teacher)

"Well begun is half done."
—Aristotle

Table of Contents

Why I Wrote This Book

I WROTE this book for the same reason you are reading it: because I love my kids.

But as a parent, I've had to swallow a cold, hard truth: my kids deserve more than just love. The Beatles were wrong when they said, "All you need is love." Most parents love their kids. Frankly, that's easy. But does love alone make you a good parent? No. Kids deserve more: you need to help them develop virtue, help them forge true friendships, and ultimately lead them to happiness. At least that's what Aristotle believed.

This is not really a parenting book. I'm not qualified to write one. I'm not going to say spanking is good or bad, or that video games are OK or not OK. Rather, I am going to use philosophy to help you understand how your kid can become virtuous, how he can develop true friendships, and what will truly make him happy. I'll leave the specifics to your better judgment.

This book is a philosophy book for parents. Sounds boring, doesn't it? But if you are a reasonably good parent, you *already are* a philosopher.

Philosophy is nothing more than the love of wisdom (*philosophia*). This book shows the real, practical connection between the ancient wisdom of Aristotle and modern case studies, statistics, and the everyday life experience of raising kids. If you're seeking wisdom in raising your kids, keep reading.

But why Aristotle? Born in 384 BC in Greece, Aristotle was a student of the famous Plato, who was a student of Socrates. He was bald. He had thin legs, small eyes, and spoke with a lisp. (He obviously made it with his brain, not his good looks.) His father, Nicomachus, was the court physician to Amyntas II (Alexander the Great's grandfather). Aristotle was probably destined to be a doctor himself and may have practiced medicine to some extent. His father's profession must have been a positive influence on Aristotle's appreciation of the sciences. He is renowned for his work in physics, biology, zoology, politics, dramatic arts, economics, ethics, and more. In short, he wrote on everything from insects to constitutions—and every one of his works is considered a masterpiece. That is quite a résumé.

Perhaps the most influential thing Aristotle did, however, was tutor Alexander the Great until the age of sixteen, at which time Alexander began to conquer the known world. It's no coincidence that the greatest emperor (who was a child himself) had the greatest teacher of all time. Many of the same lessons he must have taught to the emperor are contained in these pages.

Aristotle was concerned with human nature more than anything else. In order to become virtuous and happy, says Aristotle, your kid must perfect this human nature *in a particular way*. And this is what you will find in these pages.

Aristotle's most famous work is called the *Nicomachean Ethics*. It was named either for his father, Nicomachus, or his only son by the same name. Essentially, Aristotle wrote a book about how to become a virtuous and happy human being. I suspect he named the work for his son as a gift, as if saying, "Son, this is your road map to happiness." But whether named for his father or his son, *Ethics* is parenting advice to all future generations. It is exactly what he would tell parents because it is what he, as a parent, wanted his son to know.

But what if his son Nicomachus lived in 2012? Would Aristotle say the same things to him? YES. Absolutely. No doubt about it. How can we be so sure? Because everything he said was about the unchangeable human nature that every kid possesses. The current existence of Xbox and Facebook and iPods don't change this. We must apply his principles to the modern world, but the principles are the same today as they've always been.

If you haven't read the *Ethics*, put it on your bucket list. Aristotle will richly reward your efforts. His philosophical diction and terms can take some getting used to, though—which is one reason I wrote this book. *If Aristotle's Kid Had an iPod* translates Aristotle's concepts and arguments into contemporary language, serving as a fast-paced guide to the *Ethics* and preparing readers to tackle the great work itself.

All right, so Aristotle makes sense. Now, why me?

I don't talk much about myself in the pages of this book, primarily because the book isn't about me. It's about Aristotle, your kid, and you. I'm not a psychologist. I'm not a therapist. I'm not a world-class philosopher. Heck, I don't even have teenagers yet. So who am I?

My wife and I married young and started having babies. We have eight children. Our oldest is ten. No twins. Just one after the other. We understand Rug Rats pretty well, and I've found that Aristotle provides some excellent advice.

I'm a mediocre philosopher who is fed up with hearing stupid parenting advice and watching parents get pulverized by their kids. Every time I see a kid pitch a royal fit in public, every time I see parents succumb to their children's demands (as if *they* are Alexander the Great), every time I see parents do the *exact opposite* of what should be done, I think to myself, "They need a good dose of Aristotle." Well, here it is.

When I was studying philosophy in graduate school, I noticed that Aristotle's concepts—of moderation, habit formation, friendship, pleasure versus happiness, and so on—were very helpful in raising my three little kids. As most young parents do, I poked around at parent books and concluded that most of them stink. The best advice for raising kids was coming from 350 BC, not from the 1969 pot-smoking Woodstock psychology that has overtaken the parenting section of your local bookstore.

I have a passion for finding how philosophy applies to modern-day life. I love experiments and statistics, and every time I see one, it's as if the underlying philosophical principle oozes off the page. I find this stuff interesting, practical, exciting, and I'm convinced you can have the same experience.

Aristotle wasn't a saint. Neither am I, and neither are you. But he was keenly aware of what you, as a parent, need to do to help your kid become virtuous and happy.

One last note on this book: it isn't for the faint of heart. It's filled with hilarious stuff, but also serious stuff. It will challenge your self-assurance about how "good" your kid really is, what he's capable of doing, and how quickly things can go wrong. Sorry, but the truth hurts. Yet the greater point of the book is how magnificent your kid's life can be. If your kid seeks the path of virtue, he will be filled with peace. If he seeks true friendships, he will find more joy in giving than in receiving. And ultimately, if he is virtuous and possesses a true friend, your kid will gain true happiness, a happiness far beyond any notion of pleasure or amusement that the modern world offers.

The answers to your most important questions as a parent are best found in looking back to ancient Greece. It is my hope that once you see how nice a place it is to visit, you will stay there.

— Part I —

Virtue

"Excellence is an art won by training and habituation. . . . Excellence, then, is not an act but a habit."

—Aristotle

CHAPTER ONE

Aristotle and the Dog Whisperer

"ALL MEN BY NATURE DESIRE TO KNOW."
—ARISTOTLE

How to Become a Kid Whisperer

CESAR MILLAN is the Dog Whisperer. He begins every show with the words, "I rehabilitate dogs. I train people." Cesar's clients love their dogs but have no idea how to control them. You see it on their faces. They're exhausted. They've tried everything. But their dogs have taken over their lives.

In order to love their little pup, they must look past the growling and dodge the nipping at their heels, forgive the torn-up leather sofas, and rearrange their schedules so they can take Fido for his walk when no one else can or will.

When Cesar comes in the front door, everything changes. The dogs usually begin the same dominant routine—barking, biting, or "playful" jumping—but within seconds become submissive to this mysterious little man.

Sometimes they lean back on their hind legs, suspiciously watching Cesar's every move. Sometimes they test him, treating him like they've treated all the other humans in their lives. But amazingly, they quickly back down,

For anyone watching Cesar at work, one thing is abundantly clear: something has been communicated that we humans cannot hear.

*　　*　　*

"Calm and assertive," Cesar says in nearly every episode. "Not aggressive." His body language communicates something humans can't perceive, like a dog whistle undetected by human ears. He is instantly, almost imperceptibly, in control.

The dog owners are a different story. Watching these troubled owners is like watching *Planet of the Apes*. Cesar's clients are held hostage by their own pets. They have tried reading books, they have tried positive reinforcement, they have tried changing the environment. They have tried everything except common sense. And the Dog Whisperer is overflowing with good old-fashioned common sense.

Cesar's job is simple: convince his clients that they are humans and that their dogs are dogs.

Sounds easy, doesn't it? But in practice, it's difficult, because over many months and even years the owners have elevated their dogs to the status of humans.

The dog is "part of the family." Maybe so. But the dog doesn't want a family: it wants a pack. It doesn't want a mommy and a daddy: it wants an Alpha Male. A pack and a family are not the same thing. A daddy and an Alpha Male are not the same thing.

Some owners love to call their dogs "my baby." But no matter how much they want their puppies to be their babies, no matter how much they pamper and cuddle them, the owners must learn that the puppies will always be dogs. Dogs have doggy natures, not human natures.

Common sense tells us that if a dog has a doggy nature, it can only be happy in a doggy way. Cesar knows what makes a dog happy. He understands that a dog doesn't get happiness the same way humans do. But for some reason, the owners on *Dog Whisperer* forget this. The result: petrified, embarrassed owners and malcontent dogs.

*　*　*

Do these crazy dog owners sound like any parents you know?

Walk into any grocery store and chances are good you'll find parents petrified and embarrassed by their children, just as Cesar's clients are petrified by their dogs.

You can see the fear in mom's eyes when her kid goes on a tirade in the store, making it impossible to shop. She becomes submissive, and her kid becomes the Alpha Male. With an embarrassed smile, she says, "Oh, he's just independent," or "He has so much energy," or my favorite "He's a very strong-willed child." That might be true. But maybe Mom has the same problem that Cesar's clients have: *she has failed to understand her child's nature.*

Flummoxed dog owners call in Cesar Millan because he understands doggy nature. Likewise, parents at their wits end need to call in someone who understands human nature. They need a "Kid Whisperer."

Luckily, just such a Kid Whisperer exists, an expert whose writings on human nature are unsurpassed after nearly 2,400 years. I'm referring, of course, to Aristotle, whom we are going to come to know very well in the course of this book.

Both Cesar Millan and Aristotle understand that for any being its *nature* is the most fundamental thing.

If you want to be a successful dog owner, you need to understand doggy nature and play by its rules. Likewise, if you want to be a successful parent, you need to understand *human* nature and play by its rules.

Failure to know the nature of the creatures you interact with will lead to disastrous results . . . as Roy Horn discovered on a fateful October night in 2003

Don't Shoot the Cat!

"Don't shoot the cat!" Roy Horn murmured as he was transported to the University of Nevada Medical Center. The mad dash to the hospital was the result of the first serious injury in more than five thousand shows that Siegfried Fischbacher and Roy Horn performed together.

The German-born duo met in 1959 when they found work on the same German ocean liner. Siegfried was a trained magician, specializing as an illusionist. Roy grew up with exotic animals. This dynamic combination of magic and wild animals came alive when Roy smuggled a cheetah named Chico aboard the vessel, giving them an opportunity to connect the dots for what was to come.

Five thousand shows later, they were still performing, widely famous for spell-binding performances with White Lions and White Tigers. The "Masters of the Impossible" became the most visited show in Las Vegas.

Their performance on October 3, 2003, at the Mirage in Las Vegas started out as a typical show. But as Roy and his seven-year-old male tiger Montecore performed their routine, something went wrong. Former Mirage owner Steven Wynn, who hired the duo in 1990, reported that a woman in the front row with a "big hairdo" distracted Montecore and foolishly reached out to pet him. Roy jumped between the woman and Montecore but slipped and fell.

Roy had raised Montecore since he was a cub. They had performed together for more than six years. Montecore was as domesticated as tigers come. But Montecore, a star of the Vegas stage, was still a tiger after all.

According to eyewitnesses and as reported in the *Las Vegas Review Journal*, after disobeying a command to lie down, Montecore took a "playful swat" at Horn, causing him to lose hold of the chain around the tiger's neck.

When Horn lunged to get back control of the chain, and of Montecore, Montecore sunk his teeth into Horn's arm. Roy desperately began to hit the tiger with his microphone stand. The striking caused Montecore to release Horn's arm, but only in favor of the performer's neck. The tiger then dragged Horn offstage, teeth firmly plunged into Horn's neck, until an alert stagehand sprayed a fire extinguisher in Montecore's face.

According to Wynn and Siegfried and Roy, Montecore treated Roy as he might a tiger cub, grabbing it by the scruff of the neck and taking it to safety. Perhaps, although it seems this was more a classic case of roughhousing gone awry. It's all fun and games until someone gets mauled to within an inch of his life by a giant Siberian tiger.

No matter the final cause, it's clear this horrific event was perfectly in keeping with what tigers *do*; with what they *are*. Whatever the reason Montecore attacked that night, it's in a tiger's nature to protect, or play. But it's not in their nature to do either with humans. That's when things go wrong.

Horn was critically injured. He suffered severe blood loss, a stroke and partial paralysis. During a procedure called decompressive craniectomy, doctors removed 25 percent of his skull to relieve pressure on his brain. The skull fragment that was removed was inserted into a pouch in Roy's abdomen so it could be put back in Roy's head at a later date.

Roy was lucky to be alive and had a very long recovery in front of him. Thankfully, by 2006 Roy was up and walking around.

The Dog Whisperer and the Master of the Impossible

No one knows more about dogs than Cesar Millan. And probably no one knows more about white tigers than Roy Horn

But there is a difference between the Master of the Impossible and the Dog Whisperer. Cesar Millan is not a showman. He doesn't perform magic tricks. He knows that a dog must be treated like a dog.

More important, he knows that a human must be treated like a human.

Nowhere is Millan's philosophy of nature shown more clearly than in episode 1 of season 2 of the *Dog Whisperer*—an episode made famous by author Malcom Gladwell in his bestselling book *What the Dog Saw.*

In this episode, a Chihuahua named Bandit held an entire family hostage. He would bite anybody that came near him except his owner, Lori.

Bandit was from a puppy mill and had little human contact early in his life. Lori clearly had a deep connection with Bandit. He, in his own doggy way, "loved" her.

"He was our baby," Lori said of Bandit, as her son, Tyler, sat on the same couch, on the other side of Bandit.

At one point, Tyler reached out to pet Bandit, who leapt, snarling at Tyler. Lori's instinct was to protect her baby: Bandit.

Cesar did not like this, not a bit. Wasn't Tyler her son? Why was the aggressor—the dog—being comforted as if he had been attacked? What must Tyler conclude about his mother and his own standing in the family?

Cesar was about as angry as he gets, but still in control.

"He owns you," he said to Lori. "It seems like you are favoring the dog, and hopefully that is not the truth. . . . If Tyler kicked the dog, you would correct him. The dog is biting your son, and you are not correcting hard enough. . . . I don't understand why you are not putting two and two together."

Cesar saw Lori refusing to accept the difference between her dog and her son; he even announced to millions of people on national television, "It's not going to work." He then added, emphatically, "I would never choose a dog over my son."

Something that Lori and many others like her, and maybe even Roy Horn, don't understand is that all things must be put in their proper place. If you elevate something beyond its natural place in the universe, it will not even prosper as it was supposed to in its proper, lower place.

The Dog Whisperer gets this.

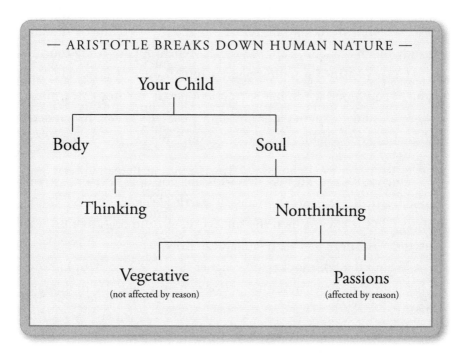

— ARISTOTLE BREAKS DOWN HUMAN NATURE —

Your Child

Body   Soul

Thinking   Nonthinking

Vegetative   Passions
(not affected by reason)   (affected by reason)

Cesar Millan understands that for a dog to be content, it must be treated as a dog. Treating a dog as a human, as Lori did, pulls the dog out of its natural state and removes all the boundaries and order that a domesticated animal needs when living on this planet with humans.

Bandit was screaming for discipline. He wanted a pack leader. He wanted the firmness of Cesar's hand. But instead, Lori caressed him like a human infant.

Would you want Lori as your pack leader? I don't think so.

Likewise, our children need to be in their proper place. I think Cesar Millan would understand that . . . and Tyler certainly understands that.

But it's not just about making sure you treat your kid as higher than your dog. It's also about understanding your kid as a human kid. Knowing what he needs and when he needs it.

Your kid must recognize that he's a kid, not a dog . . . but he's also not your drinking buddy. Just as Bandit needs the firm and steady touch of Cesar, your kid needs your firm and steady touch.

Cesar Millan is a philosopher: a philosopher of dogs. He has sought and found wisdom—at least as it pertains to dogs. And after years of study, experimentation, and practice, he has concluded something remarkable: that a dog is a dog. We can learn a lot from Cesar.

But we've also learned that kids are not dogs. A calm, stern touch; a firm demeanor; and a well-practiced tilt of the head don't always do the trick. When the subject turns from dogs to kids, we need a little more heft than Millan can offer.

We need a philosopher of a higher order. We need a philosopher who is an expert not only in doggy nature, but also in human nature.

We need Aristotle.

In the rest of this book, we'll apply Aristotle's principles and his many years of thought about virtue, friendship, and human nature to raising our kids. What *would* Aristotle do if his kid had an iPod?

For now, suffice it to say, if Aristotle had a DVR, he'd record every episode of *Dog Whisperer*.

And if he went to Vegas, he wouldn't waste his time or his money on Siegfried and Roy.

Chapter One: *Playlist*

▸ To be a Kid Whisperer, you have to understand human nature.

▸ Dogs love Cesar Millan because he treats them like dogs.

▸ You cannot train away an animal's nature.

▸ And you cannot train away your kid's nature— you must embrace it.

CHAPTER TWO

A Rational Animal

"YOUNG PEOPLE ARE IN A CONDITION
LIKE PERMANENT INTOXICATION."
—ARISTOTLE

Let's Get Meta-Physical

TO WORK with something successfully, you must understand its nature. The carpenter knows the nature of a saw is to cut. A soldier knows the nature of a gun is to shoot. The ancient philosophers made it their priority to understand the nature of all around them. Chief among these philosophers was Aristotle, who sought to understand the nature of plants, animals, government, and many things the human eye cannot see. Knowledge of these many different natures taught Aristotle that human nature is unique among all creatures.

Aristotle considered a creature's physical *and* nonphysical attributes. In his *Physics*, Aristotle probed many physical laws we now take for granted. What does it mean "to be" something? What does it mean to change from one thing to another? What is movement?

Who was the First Mover? Cutting-edge scientists are still asking these questions.

Aristotle also knew there was something more than the physical world. The study of the world "beyond" the physical is called "*meta*-physics" because *meta* means "beyond." Unfortunately, our scientific advancements distract us from the important questions of metaphysics. The more iPods and iPhones and iPads we have, the more distracted we are. The ancient philosophers, however, saw the importance of both the physical and the metaphysical world.

Aristotle was not the first to study metaphysics. Socrates before him put the subject at the forefront of philosophy. He asked questions about the human soul, its health, and its life after death. He sought wisdom and virtue in all he did, even to the point of preferring death to committing an unjust act. Socrates's execution is one of the most famous events in human history.

In 399 BC, Socrates was brought before the Greek tribunals on bogus charges of corrupting the youth and not worshiping the gods of the state. In reality, many of the movers and shakers of Athens were angry with Socrates for debunking their fallacious philosophies, making them look foolish, and even winning over friends and family. He was convicted by many of the same men who accused him and sentenced to death. His pupils bribed the guards to let him escape, but he preferred to serve his sentence than commit a crime. "It is better to suffer injustice than to commit it," he said.

Socrates reached great levels of purity and goodness without the aid of divine revelation. (Moses didn't swing by Athens with the Ten Commandments, so Socrates was a little shortchanged in his pursuit of Judeo-Christian virtue.) This shows the great power of human reason.

As a parent, you must ask yourself a serious question: do you believe it is better for your child to suffer injustice than to commit it? Which do you fear more: bodily or spiritual injury? It's much easier to agree with Socrates's axiom than to live by it. But challenging yourself with such a question is worth the time. Think about all you do for your child's physical safety. How much do you do for his spiritual safety?

Some basic metaphysics can help you care for your kid's soul. It's not as scary as it sounds, especially when Aristotle the Kid Whisperer is on your side. Aristotle was a great teacher. He was even handpicked to teach the emperor's son: Alexander the Great! By applying the principles in this book, your kid can have the same teacher as Alexander the Great!

Animal + Reason = Human

Dr. Karen Wynn is a developmental psychologist and holds a doctorate from M.I.T. Her studies have taken her to many prestigious universities; more important, she's made great strides in understanding the age-old question, what's going on in that baby's head? I'm sure you've asked it many times. Your infant starts laughing or being goofy or looking around quizzically. What's he thinking?

In the early '90s, Dr. Wynn conducted a series of studies with five-month-old babies at the University of Arizona. By using screens and Mickey Mouse figurines, and judging the babies' reaction when one or several figurines was added or subtracted, she concluded that babies could actually understand basic math . . . or at least they knew when something was wrong.

Wynn and her team placed a figure of Mickey Mouse on a table in front of the babies. Then she put a screen in front of the figurine, and in total view of the infant, a second Mickey Mouse was placed behind the screen. The screen was then removed, and cameras recorded how long the infant stared at the figurines on the table. In other instances, either no additional figurines were added or two more were added. In these cases, the babies consistently stared for several seconds longer, indicating that they knew that something had gone mathematically wrong. One plus one had not equaled two. And the babies knew something was up.

Dr. Wynn was adamant in her findings: "Infants can compute the results of simple arithmetic problems." Aristotle was adamant in his findings as well: your kid is a rational animal, and on a certain level, he is rational from the very beginning. It just takes a little while to get from Mickey Mouse math to calculus.

— THE MORAL LIFE OF BABIES —

Dr. Karen Wynn now runs Yale's Infant Cognition Center, and she is making great breakthroughs in showing that babies are actually pretty smart.

As we've seen, they can understand basic math, but they can also make moral judgments, read facial cues, and much more.

For more, go to:
www.yale.edu/infantlab

*   *   *

There's no evidence that Aristotle used figurines of iconic cartoon characters in his inquiry into human nature. But he would have fundamentally agreed with Dr. Wynn's findings. In his *Metaphysics*, Aristotle referred to humans as *"zoon logon echon,"* or "animals with a rational principle," where *principle* means something like "governing entity." Everything has a principle: plants, animals, governments, and humans. After Aristotle studied every known creature, he concluded that the primary distinction between humans and other creatures is the principle of reason. Reason is our governing principle. Not instinct, not emotions, but reason.

This is true for your kid, despite the fact that he jams forks into electric sockets, drinks toilet water, and paints on the wall with poop. Why would nine-year-olds try to determine how far a bungee cord can stretch between them? Or why might a teenager rollerblade while holding on to the bumper of a car? The answer is that having a rational nature and always *being rational* are not the same thing.

Aristotle compares your kid's nature to an acorn. It has the potential to develop into an oak tree but needs water, sunshine, and fertile soil. If you expose an acorn only to cold and darkness, or if you bury it in barren ground, it will remain an acorn and never develop. Your kid's rational nature is similar. She has the potential to develop into a rational and virtuous person, someone who has true friendships and is truly happy. But she needs certain things. Like the acorn, she needs physical things: water, sunshine, and food. But as a human, she needs metaphysical things as well: virtue, friendship, and happiness.

Before we move on to these metaphysical things, let's look at how Aristotle compares your kid to physical things, like plants and animals.

Vegging Out

You can see Aristotle's "totem pole" of nature in your home. Your potted plant is at the bottom, your dog is in the middle, and your kid is on top. A dog contains all the essential attributes of a plant (thus a dog is a plant) and humans contain all the essential attributes of a dog and a plant (thus the human is both an animal and a plant).

Aristotle explains that plants grow, need sunlight, water, and nutrients from the ground. But plants have no emotion or reason. You could curse at a flower all day and it won't hold a grudge.

Likewise, your kid grows and needs nourishment. His body,

like that of a plant, functions without thought or intentionality. He doesn't think about blinking or breathing or beating his heart. When you see your kid sleeping, notice the vegetative attributes: he is growing, living off oxygen, his digestive system is working (which is why he needs a Pull-Up). When you see your lazy teenager napping on the couch, remember that he is literally "vegging out."

The next rung up the totem pole we find your dog. It grows, eats, and drinks, but also has traits beyond that of plants. Aristotle calls these traits "appetites" or "passions."

The passions are similar to emotions or feelings.* Think of a dog's passions, causing him to jump the fence when the Dame down the street is in heat. These passions are very strong in your dog and your kid.

Many people say that passions are bad. Aristotle would say, "On the contrary. They are very good!" Passions make things go. They serve as fuel in your kid's engine. Without them, there'd be little motivation to do anything. But too much fuel injection, if not directed in the right direction, can lead your kid right off a cliff. This is why God gave him a built-in GPS: his reason. This is the defining difference between your kid and all other creatures in this world. Unfortunately, the people in Seattle don't seem to understand this.

Yuppies and Their Puppies

Phillip Longman is a professional demographer at the New America Foundation and a former senior writer for *U.S. News & World Report*. Longman is an expert in the reasons behind, and the consequences of, people having fewer children.

"What's the difference between Seattle and Salt Lake City?" he

---

* Throughout this book, I will use *appetite, passion, emotions,* and *feelings* interchangeably. For the most part, they are.

asks in his article "The Liberal Baby Bust." "In Seattle, there are nearly 45% more dogs than children. In Salt Lake City, there are nearly 19% more kids than dogs."

There's nothing wrong with having a dog. There is nothing wrong per se with not having children. But there's something wrong with thinking that a dog can replace having children Why can't a dog fill the void? Why can't a woman pick up a pooch from the pound and avoid the problems of bearing and raising a child? Because a dog is not a rational animal.

People in Seattle are seeking meaningful relationships with irrational creatures. This is a futile attempt. Dogs have passions, instinct, and a playful manner, but not reason. Reason is the only power that enables love, forgiveness, and friendship. As a parent, you desire a lifelong relationship with your kid. This is only possible because both of you are rational beings who possess the traits unique to human nature.

Raising kids can bring you great joy *and* great pain. It's a gamble. You can't predict how things will turn out. The development of his rationality and the taming of his passions will take twists and turns beyond your imagination. And if things go wrong, you can't drop him off at the pound.

The rational power of human nature is a catch-22: it makes possible happiness and misery; it enables your kid to love you and break your heart. But most important, reason can lead your child to true friendships and happiness. In the next chapter, C. S. Lewis, author of *The Chronicles of Narnia*, will help us understand the relation between your kid's passions and his reason.

Chapter Two: *Playlist*

▸ Go "beyond" the physical. That's where to find the most important things in your child's life.

▸ Remember the acorn. Your kid is a rational animal but has to develop.

▸ Remember the totem poll. Creation has a hierarchy, and Aristotle places your kid at the top.

▸ No rational nature = no deep relationship. People in Seattle will be very lonely.

CHAPTER THREE

Kids without Chests

"YOUNG PEOPLE OVERDO EVERYTHING;
THEY LOVE TOO MUCH, HATE TOO MUCH,
AND THE SAME WITH EVERYTHING ELSE!"
—ARISTOTLE

Vulcans and Stoics at the Playground

THINK HOW boring planet Vulcan must be. It is home to an extraterrestrial humanoid species in the *Star Trek* universe. The most famous Vulcan is Mr. Spock, second in command of the *Enterprise* to Captain James T. Kirk. Through meditation, Vulcans suppress all emotions and are directed by logic alone.

Vulcans are superior to humans in many ways. Because of Planet Vulcan's stronger gravity, they have the strength of three men. They are more intelligent. They live much longer than humans, sometimes reaching 220 years old. And because their planet is essentially a big desert, they can survive without water for a long time.

It's a common misconception that Vulcans lack emotion when in fact they have a natural tendency toward extreme emotion. A

Vulcan is the last person you want to tick off. As the saying goes, "Beware the fury of a patient man."

How would you like a bunch of Vulcan kids at your son's eighth birthday party? It'd be more boring than a bingo game in a retirement home. You don't want your kid to act like a Vulcan, and you don't want him to be best friends with one. Emotions are good and should not be suppressed.

The twenty-fourth-century Vulcans are a fictional race, but back in Greece in the third century BC, a real sort of Vulcan arose. Zeno of Citium began a movement called Stoicism. He saw the evil that resulted from anger, lust, and greed. The Stoics therefore aimed for a state called *apatheia*, or "apathy." Imagine a life drained of all emotion: no temper tantrums from your two-year-old; no drama-queen episodes from your teenage daughter. Wouldn't life be easier without this baggage?

It was a nice idea, but the Stoics couldn't pull it off. Such a fad will never last. We *are* emotional creatures. We can't avoid our emotions; we need to embrace them and direct them toward the good.

You don't want your kid growing up to be like Mr. Spock or Zeno. You want your kid to have an emotional life that helps him be happy. This is only possible by directing emotions in a proper way, not by suppressing them.

Aristotle believes a parent must do more than educate, feed, and clothe. You must also teach your kid how to "feel" the right way, including how to laugh, cry, and even get really angry.

Teaching Kids to Laugh, Cry, and Get Really Ticked Off

Imagine how "refined" and "sophisticated" Oxford University was when C. S. Lewis was teaching there in the mid-twentieth century. If a kid was to meet the expectations of the day, training had to start early. Prep schools made kids grow up fast. Rigorous academic and social refinement was the norm. There was little time for play. Sounds like planet Vulcan. Lewis favored good education, social manners, and a refined culture but knew that too much rigidity was unnatural.

In his classic book *The Abolition of Man*, Lewis took on teachers who tried to drive emotions out of their students. "My own experience as a teacher," Lewis says, "tells an opposite tale. For every one pupil who needs to be guarded from a weak excess of sensibility there are three who need to be awakened from the slumber of cold vulgarity." In other words, kids need the *right* emotions, not a lack of emotions. Educators and parents should not "cut down jungles" of emotions, as Lewis describes it, but rather "irrigate deserts" of apathy.

Lewis had a high regard for the passions ("the gut") but knew they needed direction. He had a high regard for reason ("the head") but knew it needed help getting things done. To unite the head and the gut, Lewis argued, men need "chests," the place where reason and passion come together. By uniting reason and his passions, man can "feel" in the right way.

Your kid is a discombobulated mess right now, precisely because he's sorting out the crazy thoughts whirling in his head and the crazy passions whirling in his gut.

— ARISTOTLE UPHOLDS EMOTIONS —

Aristotle wrote his *Poetics* in response to Plato's works that dismissed poetry and drama for inciting the emotions of the audience.

Aristotle believed that this stirring of the emotions was a good thing. He even coined a term for it: *catharsis*, meaning the purification of emotions.

whirling in his gut. He doesn't need a lobotomy; he needs emotional direction. Give it to him.

It is futile to attempt to suppress emotion, but it is also foolish to leave the emotions undeveloped. Modern society says we have no control over emotion. There are endless excuses for bad behavior in the classroom. There's always a lurking disorder that medication must solve. In Lewis's day, teachers bore the kidsd to death, and now we drug them to death. Your kid deserves more.

It's your job to train your kid emotionally, just like you train her physically and intellectually. The right emotion in the right amount can *literally* save your life, as one dad learned from his five-year-old son.

* * *

On April 20, 1990, five-year-old Stevie Walker and his dad were at home alone. Dad was making dinner and told little Stevie to go down to the basement and turn on a movie. "I'll be down in just a minute."

Stevie went downstairs and started watching his movie, but a few minutes later, he heard a loud crash. He turned around to see his dad laying at the bottom of the stairs. His dad was unconscious at the foot of the steps. "Dad," Stevie said a few times. "Dad, are you joking? Daddy, are you joking?" He squatted down, nudged him gently with his finger, and said, "Daddy, are you OK?" No response. Stevie pushed him harder. No response.

Stevie was still not sure what was wrong. He was only five. But when he saw blood starting to seep from his dad's mouth, Stevie knew this was not good. Then he saw blood pooling out from beneath his dad's head. Something clicked in Stevie's mind: Daddy isn't joking.

Here he was: a five-year-old boy with his father unconscious and bleeding from the mouth and head. He was all alone. For most kids, the fear would be paralyzing. Did he think about waiting for mommy to come home? Did he cry? Did he get angry at his dad?

We'll never know all the answers, but we know what Stevie did.

He walked up the stairs, pulled his little chair across the kitchen floor, climbed up to the telephone, and called 911. He told the operator that his dad was lying on the ground and wouldn't get up, that he had blood coming from his mouth and the back of his head, and that his mommy was not home.

The operator told him to check to see if his father was breathing. Putting his little fingers under his dad's nose, Stevie reported back that, yes, he felt air coming out. The operator then instructed him to look for something he could hold against the wound to stop the bleeding. Thankfully, by this time the paramedics had arrived.

As they loaded Stevie's dad up in the ambulance, one of them knelt down, grasped Stevie's little arms, and said, "You did the right thing. You have probably saved your daddy's life." And in fact, he did save his life. Stevie's father suffered severe head trauma with a large laceration across the back of his skull. He was hospitalized for eight days but recovered fully.

During an interview, Stevie had a remarkable insight. "If you wanta be good and pretty special, then you gotta do what you gotta do." I'm not sure Aristotle could have put it any better.

Stevie was scared, but not too scared. He thought his dad might be joking, but he wasn't sure. He was scared enough to call 911, but brave enough to follow the operator's directions.

Aristotle—and C. S. Lewis—would be very proud of Stevie. He had the perfect emotional response to a very scary situation. Maybe your five-year-old can't analyze complex fact patterns, but he *can* feel the right feelings. He can be scared of snakes. He can be scared of getting hit by a car. He can regret hurting another person.

Despite what a relativist may say—and there are a bunch of relativists out there—there are morally good and bad emotions at certain times. "I can't help my feelings" is incorrect.

Stevie didn't say, "You gotta think the right thought." He said that if you have a desire to be good—"If you wanta be good and pretty special"—then you have simply to act. You must respond, as opposed to thinking everything through. Our emotions come in handy here, especially for little kids who can't fully rely on their intellectual powers. Passions can be your kid's greatest asset. But you must help him develop a "chest," as C. S. Lewis would say.

Stevie was a kid with a chest. His mind knew the right thing, and his gut had the normal fears any kid would have. Most important, his "chest" filtered the emotions and allowed his mind to direct those fears in the right direction.

Chapter Three: *Playlist*

- ▶ Vulcans and Stoics reject emotions as bad. They would be very boring playmates for your kid.

- ▶ Your emotions are not like your appendix: you actually need them to be happy!

- ▶ "Kids without Chests":
    - ▷ Head = Reason
    - ▷ Gut = Passion
    - ▷ Chest = Passions guided by Reason

- ▶ As C. S. Lewis says, don't "cut down the jungles" of your kid's emotions but rather "irrigate the deserts."

CHAPTER FOUR

The Four Moral Characters

"OUR CHARACTERS ARE A RESULT
OF OUR CONDUCT."

—ARISTOTLE

ONCE UPON a time, Socrates, Frodo the Hobbit, King David, and Darth Vader were having dinner at the Cheesecake Factory. After a good meal and great conversation, it was time for dessert. Their waitress was worn out from keeping King David and Darth Vader happy but was comforted by a smile from Socrates, who paid more attention to the staff than to his own dinner party.

The Cheesecake Factory had countless dessert options but was best known for its signature raspberry cheesecake, topped with a raspberry glaze and a bit of whip cream. "You cannot go wrong with this," the waitress explained. "Everyone LOVES IT!" She slowly walked around the table as each guest admired it.

"Shall we begin with you, Mr. Socrates?"

"Oh, no thank you, my child," Socrates said.

"But Mr. Socrates," the waitress replied, "you rarely enjoy a nice dessert. Surely you can indulge every now and then."

"No thank you," Socrates repeated. "I haven't eaten sweets in years. I no longer desire it. My soup and garden salad hit the spot."

The waitress gave in with a look of dejection.

"How about you, Mr. Frodo?" she asked. "Shall I bring a piece for you?"

"Oh dear," he said as he rubbed his chin in deliberation. Hobbits always have room for dessert.

"Well, uh," he stuttered. "It looks delicious. And I love cheesecake. But, well, Gandalf told me to be more temperate, a virtue that doesn't come easily to Hobbits."

After struggling for a moment, Frodo leaned back in his chair and folded his hands as his mind and body came back into order. "No thank you. I shall pass."

She then turned to King David, who sat high in his chair with great nobility. It seemed natural to him. She imagined that he looked regal even as a boy herding sheep.

"Your Highness, a king deserves a good dessert. And our head chef mentioned that he is a big fan of your psalms."

The king thought to himself. "Darn it! That wretched prophet, Nathan! He has told me to avoid any indulgence, whatever the cost. I must repent, he says, for my sins with Bathsheba. Nathan is right. I must get control of myself. I must.

"Please give my regards to your chef," King David continued, "but I must decline. I have had my plenty tonight and many other nights. Thank you."

He saw Socrates cut him a quick smile, which pleased him.

"Your Highness," the waitress persisted slyly, "if you danced before our Lord's tabernacle, why not rejoice for bringing these four companions together?" Then she lowered the piece of cake within inches of his nose.

He thought to himself, "I am shocked at her eloquence and insight." He felt his gut stir as he kept looking at the cheesecake.

"Indeed, my fair young lady. Indeed. I accept your offer, but please, only a small piece."

The waitress then turned to her final customer. Noticing Darth Vader's deep breathing, and staring straight into his dark mask, she began to say, "Excuse me, Mr. Vader. Could I interest you in . . ."

Vader replied before she could finish: "I WILL TAKE TWO."

*   *   *

The four guests at the Cheesecake Factory represent the Four Moral Characters in Aristotle's *Ethics*: The virtuous man (Socrates), the strong-willed man (Frodo), the weak-willed (King David), and the vicious (Darth Vader). We'll discuss these Four Moral Characters in depth in just a bit

You are reading this book because you are interested in your kid's character development. Your child's development is the unfolding of an ability. As with physical, mental, and social development, your kid's moral development takes hard work and persistence. As the old saying goes, "No pain, no gain." As a parent, you must reach down inside your child's character and pull the ability out. It is, in a sense, giving birth to excellence.

Socrates saw himself this way. His mother was a midwife, an image he used for his own work as a philosopher. In Socrates's day, midwives were usually barren women who helped others bring life into the world. Socrates said he was like a midwife who is barren but helps bring to life wisdom and goodness in others. Mom and dad have the same job in regards to their children.

This concept of development is vital for understanding Aristotle's Four Moral Characters. We are born with a tendency toward selfishness, violence, and all sorts of vice. This tendency is called original sin. If you doubt it, just visit a day care and watch little humans scream for a juice box, steal toys, and bite their playmates.

Goodness, however, is in each of us. It is the work of a philosopher, and a parent, to help others bring this goodness to the world.

Keep in mind two points as we work through the four characters:

1. Your kid is a "rational animal," which means that she has reason *and* passion. Sometimes reason and passion get along; sometimes they don't.

2. Your kid is not simply one of the Four Moral Characters. In some areas she might be like Socrates. In others she might be like Darth Vader. But most often she is like Frodo or King David.

Let's first take a look at King David, who far too often allowed his passions to get the upper hand.

Weak-Willed King David

It was the summer of 1038 BC. The king could not sleep after a long, stressful day. He decided to take a walk on the roof to enjoy the cool night air.

As David gazed about his city, he noticed a beautiful woman in a courtyard. And she wasn't just reading the *Jerusalem Times* in a lawn chair; she was bathing. He stared. He stared longer. He thought to look away, but he didn't. Was she married, or was she fair game? His own marital status was irrelevant because he could have as many wives as he wanted. So David said to himself, "Well, I'm the king, and she's pretty hot. Why not give her a call?"

David called a servant to find out who the woman was. "Is this one Bathsheba, the wife of Uriah the Hittite?" his servant asked. Oops! She was married. David was the protector of God's law (including adultery) and supposed to set a good example. His head said "Stay away," but his gut screamed "Bring her to me!"

His reason fought a valiant fight against his passion, but in the end, his reason lost.

"Bring her to me."

It was not wrong for David to notice Bathsheba. It was wrong, however, to let the lust settle in his soul. You might say the first look belonged to God; the second belonged to David. Bathsheba came to David's room, and . . . well, you know what happened.

If Aristotle were announcing the event like a sportscaster, he would have said, "And Passion has overcome Reason, it has taken the lead, and it is now soaring ahead. Reason is nowhere to be seen!"

A couple of weeks later, King David got the news from Bathsheba: "I'm pregnant." Oops again! Faced with another moral struggle, David did exactly what your kid does when he breaks the rules: he tried to cover it up. The more our passions take over, the more our reason is suppressed. In other words, we get dumber every time we give in to a craving. Or, as the popular blogger Mark Shea says, "Sin makes us stupid."

At this point, David's passions were raging. He was angry and scared. But David had an idea. He called Uriah in from battle and "rewarded him" for his good service by allowing him to go home for the night. The idea was that Uriah would lie with his wife and claim the child as his own. At that time, however, it was considered dishonorable to lie with your wife while friends were dying on the battlefield. Uriah did not go home. He slept outside the palace rather than walking down the street to the comfort of his own bed. David then pushed harder, telling Uriah to go home. But Uriah refused.

King David then turned to Plan B: get Uriah hammered! He invited Uriah back to the palace for a party. "Surely," thought David, "now he will lose his sense of honor and hop in bed with his wife!" But Uriah still did not. He slept outside.

David was out of options. His reason struggled again with his passion. It's bad PR for the godly king to get caught cheating with his soldier's wife. His passions said to get rid of the problem. His reason said happiness would only come from doing the right thing.

But David's reason lost its struggle again, and he became *even dumber.* David wrote a letter to Uriah's commanding officer, ordering Uriah to the front line of the fiercest battle to leave him there to die. Uriah was killed. David immediately took Bathsheba for his wife so that it would not appear that the baby was conceived out of wedlock.

It is important to note that David didn't want to kill Uriah. He liked him! But when passion gets the best of us, we do things out of character. St. Paul says, "For I do not understand my own actions. For I do not do what I want, but I do the very thing I hate." Think how your kid does things out of character. "That's not like my kid!" you say to yourself.

Aristotle says that our character is built one little action at a time. Good or bad behavior doesn't happen in a vacuum. Your kid's outburst of anger is the result of smaller acts of anger. His act of kindness is the result of smaller acts of kindness.

King David's character is unfolding before our eyes. He wasn't a murderer until he was an adulterer, and he wasn't an adulterer until he was a peeping tom. He thought his plan had worked. He must have felt a sense of relief . . . until the Prophet Nathan paid him a visit and told him the following story: There were two men in one city, one was rich and one was poor. The rich man had many flocks and herds. The poor man had but one little lamb. He loved this lamb like a child. The rich man had a visitor one day and, instead of killing one of his many lambs for a meal, he stole and killed the poor man's lamb.

David became enraged. "This man will surely die!" he yelled. Nathan then looked deep into the King's eyes and proclaimed,

"This man is you." David was confused. What? How could this be?" Nathan then explained that David had stolen the one that Uriah loved when he had countless others of his own.

Like a thunderbolt, the reality of what he had done hit him. He hated men like himself. God punished men like himself. "How have I gotten myself into this mess?" he thought. "What have I become?" Remorse overcame him. And for the rest of his life, he regretted his actions.

*   *   *

The story of King David and Bathsheba show us many things about Aristotle's weak-willed person:

1. There is a struggle between reason and the passions.
2. The passions win.
3. The person does not so much *choose* to be bad but *gives in*, or *breaks under pressure*.
4. The person feels remorse and repents.

David demonstrated all these traits. His struggle began on the rooftop, where he had the chance to walk away but didn't. His passions had one little victory after another until he did something unthinkable. But he wasn't embracing evil; he was breaking under pressure. And finally, on seeing the truth of what he had become, he felt remorse and repented.

At times, your kid will be like King David. Hopefully he won't go as far as David did, but the process will be the same. From the earliest ages, kids learn how to struggle with passions. Perhaps stealing a cookie out of the cookie jar is the quintessential example of a kid struggling between what he *knows* to be right and what he *wants* to do. An in-depth study has been performed on children's ability to withstand this temptation. The results are surprising to us but wouldn't be to Aristotle.

*   *   *

In 1972 psychologist Walter Mischel of Stanford University performed one of the most successful (and funny) behavioral experiments in history. Through his psychological studies of different levels of self-control in different ethnic groups, Mischel learned that, despite stereotypes, ethnicity had nothing to do with self-control, while social and economic backgrounds did. He then wanted to understand better how self-control developed in children, focusing particularly on "deferred gratification," the ability to wait to get what you want.

Mischel's "Marshmallow Experiment" was held in the Bing Nursery School at Stanford University using children ages four to six. The children were placed in an empty room with a single chair and table without any distractions. They were allowed to choose a marshmallow, an Oreo cookie, or a pretzel stick, which was placed on the table. They were told that if they waited fifteen minutes, they would get a second marshmallow (or cookie or pretzel).

Aristotle would have loved watching the children try to resist the temptation. It perfectly illustrates the internal struggle we all face between reason and passion. "Here," reason says, "just wait fifteen minutes and get a second treat," whereas the passion says, "Come on! Just eat it. It'll be so delicious. You don't need a second one anyway."

I can see Aristotle behind the glass window, watching the children, laughing alongside Mischel as he saw the kids "cover their eyes with their hands or turn around so that they can't see the tray," as Michel reported. "[O]thers start kicking the desk, or tug on their pigtails, or stroke the marshmallow as if it were a tiny stuffed animal."

More than six hundred children participated in this experiment, and only a small minority ate the marshmallow immediately. According to Aristotle, this is because only a small percentage of people are virtuous or vicious. Now, he wouldn't say these kids were vicious per se, but it appears these kids didn't even struggle and simply went directly after the object of their desire. King David didn't do this. He struggled. If little Darth Vader was in the experiment, he would have eaten it immediately.

Two-thirds of the kids attempted to wait the fifteen minutes but gave in. These are the weak-willed kids. They had good intentions, but they broke under pressure. This is a very important point about the weak-willed child: they are not trying to be bad. On the contrary, they are trying to be good but have not yet developed the willpower to do so.

This experiment has been performed many times since 1972. Hilarious modern versions of the experiment can be found on YouTube. But the important factor of the 1972 experiment is that follow-up studies have been able to see how those original six hundred children turned out. Did the strong-willed turn out any different from the weak-willed? Surprisingly, to the experts, yes. But again, Aristotle wouldn't be surprised at all.

The first follow-up study was in 1988, when the kids were sixteen. The kids with greater self-control were described more than ten years later by their parents as "significantly more competent." In 1990 these same children had higher SAT scores. In 2011 the same characteristics proved to have remained with the participants well into adulthood.

Aristotle and the Marshmallow Experiment both explain that how we choose our dessert at the Cheesecake Factory as adults is largely dependent on whether we put our hand in the cookie jar as a kid. It is a temptation, however, for modern parents to say, "My kid can't help himself." Aristotle would call BS.

As a parent, you are like the prophet Nathan. When your kid caves in, it's because he's weak like King David was weak. You have to hold the mirror up to your kid's face, like Nathan did for David.

When he show signs of remorse, rejoice! All he needs is a little help in getting through the next struggle.

As a child grows older, he may not be nibbling the very edge of a marshmallow, but he may be nibbling on a girl's neck in the backseat, or looking over a classmate's shoulder on exam day, or taking just one puff of a joint. As an adult, you know that your "marshmallows" can become very serious, as King David found out.

— A NOTE ON TERMS —

Aristotle vs. James Dobson

Chances are you've heard of Dr. James Dobson. He's had a positive influence on parents throughout the world. That's why it's important to note here some unfortunate terminology.

If Aristotle were to read Dr. Dobson's book on the strong-willed child, he might agree with Dr. Dobson's underlying concepts, but he wouldn't like the term strong-willed. For Dr. Dobson, a strong-willed child is one that stubbornly challenges authority. According to Aristotle, this definition is more fitting for weak-willed. Nonetheless, Dr. Dobson deserves praise, not blame.

You've heard it a thousand times. Little Johnny ignores his mom's pleas to stop writing on the walls. "Johnny, we don't draw on the walls, we draw on paper." Johnny, pulling the cap off a fresh marker, turns and grins at mom before adding a couple of lines of blue to the dining room. Johnny's mom shakes her head, takes a long of sip of tea, and, sighing, says to you: "Oh, he's just so strong-willed. I think he may be an artist when he grows up."

Dr. Dobson did not intend for every wimpy parent to use his term strong-willed for their disobedient child. But unfortunately, the term has been hijacked. According to Aristotle, Johnny's not strong-willed; he's actually weak-willed . . . and pretty naughty.

I greatly admire Dr. Dobson and his work, but when it comes to this specific term, I am using strong-willed the way Aristotle would use it, not the way Dobson (or his hijackers) use it.

You have a God-given duty to help your child win the struggle between reason and passion. You have to show him that the struggle is occurring, and yet happiness and peace awaits him on the other side. The struggle is painful, but the victory is sweet—you get two marshmallows, not just one. With just a little practice, the weak-willed child can become a strong-willed child, which we will now discuss.

Strong-Willed Frodo

Frodo Baggins of the Shire was your typical Hobbit who loved to eat, smoke, and fish. He wanted a quiet life with no adventure, as every good Hobbit does. But fate would have it differently.

Frodo is one of the greatest heroes in all of literature, and yet he fails many times. Despite the presence of goblins and elves, *The Lord of the Rings* by J. R. R. Tolkien is a real story. It is the story of good and evil, nature and grace, sin and redemption. Aristotle would love it because it is also the story of the Four Moral Characters.

— MORAL CHARACTERS IN —

The Lord of the Rings

The Virtuous . . . . . . Gandalf

Strong-Willed . . . . . . Frodo

Weak-Willed . . . . Gollum

Vicious . . . . Saruman

Frodo struggles throughout his journey to Mount Doom. The Ring he carries is the source of temptation. He is tempted many times to use its power to disappear and escape danger. Despite Gandalf's warnings to never do so, Frodo's passions overcome his reason at least three times. One of these times, on a hill called Weathertop, Frodo saw the black riders approaching. He was overwhelmed with fear. He struggled. He remembered Gandalf's command, but his passions were too strong. As he felt the Ring's temptation, "he longed to yield. Not with the hope of escape, or of doing anything, either good or bad: he simply felt that he must take the Ring and put it on his finger."

The result of giving in, of being weak-willed, is a lethal blow by the Dark Riders, who stab him with a poisonous sword. He would have died but for the healing power of the Elves.

But there are other times when Frodo is strong-willed. He is tempted to slip on the Ring when the hobbits are prisoners of the Barrow-wight, but here you can see the strong-willed character at work:

> Then a wild thought of escape came to him. He wondered if he put on the Ring, whether the Barrow-wight would miss him, and he might find some way out. . . .
>
> But the courage that had been awakened in him was now too strong: he could not leave his friends so easily. He wavered, groping in his pocket, and then fought with himself again. . . . Suddenly resolve hardened in him.

This sort of struggle is present in your child's life. Frodo is a great example for them. One day your kid is good; the next day not so good. Over time, Frodo's reason became stronger, and he was able to overcome his passions. This is good, but it is not yet virtuous. Your child's journey to virtue is as long and perilous as Frodo's journey to Mount Doom.

The *Lord of the Ring* fans are saying at this point, "But Frodo failed at the end. How is he a hero? How is he strong-willed?" After a long journey in which Frodo mostly overcame his temptations, he lets us down. As he stands on the edge of Mount Doom, ready to throw the Ring into the volcano, he is overcome with passion, puts on the Ring, and tries to leave. His friend Sam can't believe his eyes. Frodo is better than this. And it is only through luck or grace that the Ring finds its way into the lava and is destroyed.

But this, too, is fitting for the strong-willed. Aristotle would say that Frodo was *not* virtuous, and that is why he failed. Frodo was not perfect. He was like you and me. The good thing about being strong-willed is that most of the time reason overcomes the passions, *but not always*. If your son or daughter has reached the state of "strong-willed" in a particular area of life, understand this: your job is not done! Your kid was made for more than the struggle. Your kid was made for virtue.

*   *   *

The strong-willed (Frodo) and weak-willed (King David) have something in common: they both struggle. There is an internal battle. Neither enjoys his current moral state. It is hard. But being virtuous, as we will see, is *easy* once you get there.

It's not all black and white when it comes to your kid's moral development. Your kid is weak-willed in some areas but strong-willed in others. Perhaps your kid is strong-willed when it comes to homework and resists the temptation to talk on the phone. Or maybe your kid is an athlete and has established good eating habits. Look at your kid's life and see where he struggles but generally ends up doing the right thing. It is in these areas that he is strong-willed and on the path to virtue.

The other side of the coin is also true. Perhaps your daughter knows that she needs to do homework but can't resist checking her phone every time it vibrates. Or perhaps your teenage son is overweight, knows it, and has tried to eat healthy, but the nighttime cravings kick in before bedtime and he splurges.

According to Aristotle, your kid can convert his weak-willed areas into strong-willed areas with proper training and influence.

It's important to remember that nothing is set in stone. Character flaws are an opportunity, not a curse or a disability. Your kid can change—and so can you.

Socrates: A Virtuous Man Is Hard to Find

The virtuous man is as hard to find as a world-class athlete. They are few and far between. But look no further. You have found him. Unfortunately, he's been dead for a couple of thousand years.

In our Cheesecake Factory story, Socrates had no desire for the dessert. Even though the waitress waved it in his face, he admired it without desiring it. Socrates made self-mastery a lifetime quest. As a young man in battle, he was tasked with holding a certain post at the most dangerous part of the battlefield. Many friends began to fall dead, and many others retreated. But not Socrates. It was his duty to guard his post, and he was willing to die to do so.

As a young man the thought of death must have scared him. Intelligent and from a wealthy family, he had a bright future ahead of him, perhaps as an influential politician. But the young Socrates of that battle was a strong-willed man on his way to becoming a virtuous man. There were countless reasons to fear death. But this young man, staring death in the face, overcame his selfish motives.

As he grew older, a friend told him that the famous Oracle of Delphi had said that Socrates was the wisest man in the world. Believing this was foolish, Socrates set off in search of a truly wise man in order to prove the Oracle wrong. He found master craftsmen from different trades but determined they were not truly wise. All the experts pretended to know what they did not.

After many attempts and failures to find a truly wise man, Socrates learned that the Oracle was right: Socrates was the wisest man in the world *because* he knew that he was not wise. This humility was the prerequisite to his virtue, as it is the prerequisite to your child's virtue. Now let's consider the other aspects of virtue.

*　*　*

King David isn't vicious, and Frodo Baggins isn't virtuous. They both struggled. But Socrates is different. He did not struggle in the Cheesecake Factory because he had struggled years ago. We can assume he had the natural tendencies every young man has. Over time, however, it became easier to overcome the temptation. Eventually, there was no temptation at all. He could look at the cheesecake, recognize its beauty, and have no desire for it. Socrates, however, didn't do this with just cheesecake. He did it with all things that hurt his soul. This is freedom.

Socrates's passions, however, were not dead. He was not a Vulcan or a Stoic. Rather, he craved all things good for his soul. The truly virtuous person—like Mother Teresa or Saint Francis— desires virtue more than you and I desire anything in our lives. That's right: the virtuous have even bigger cravings than the rest of us. There's an old story that tells us how much we must desire the virtuous life if we are to fully obtain it.

*　*　*

There was an old monk who lived a life of solitude, prayer, and fasting in the desert. Due to his prayerful self-sacrifice, he became known as a man of great wisdom. Men and women traveled long distances to seek his counsel.

A young hermit came to him one day and said, "I want to know what true holiness is. Will you teach me ?"

"Are you sure you want to know?" asked the old monk.

"I am certain," the young monk replied.

"Well, we will see. Come with me." The old monk led him to a nearby stream of flowing water.

"Kneel down in the water," the old monk instructed. The young monk did as he was told.

Suddenly, the old monk grabbed the back of the young monk's head, and thrust his face into the water. The young monk flailed his arms, trying to come up for air, but the old monk held him there until he nearly lost consciousness and then pulled him up. The young monk, terrified and confused, gasped for air. Just as he got his senses back, the old monk thrust him back into the water again. The young monk kicked and screamed under the water. But again, he was pulled up just before drowning.

After he gasped for air again and filled his lungs enough to speak, he began to ask in terror, "What are you . . ." But a third time, the old monk thrust him back into the water. It did not take long this time for the young monk to lose his breath. He felt the life slipping from him. But again, he was pulled out of the water just in time.

The old monk dragged the young monk to the bank of the stream and laid him gently on his back. He knelt down and lovingly held the young monk's head in his lap and comforted him as he came to his senses.

The young monk, still terrified but relieved the torture was over, said, "Why have you done this to me?"

The old monk looked on him with loving eyes and answered, "My child, holiness is a craving for God as much as you were just craving air to breath."

* * *

The virtuous man craves virtue with all his heart. He doesn't simply avoid vice. You must teach your kid not only to shun evil, but to also embrace good. In fact, embracing good is easier than shunning evil once you get the hang of it.

Your kid's reason and passions were made for virtue, as Socrates demonstrates in his own life. Reason and passions were made for teamwork, aiming together at truth, goodness, and beauty. When you kid desires goodness, he is more alive than ever before.

In one way, the vicious man is the opposite of the virtuous: the vicious desires evil, and the virtuous desires good. But the virtuous man and the vicious man have a lot in common. Neither the virtuous nor the vicious struggles. Their reason and passions are united. And finally, becoming vicious takes a long time, as Anakin Skywalker learned.

Darth Vader: The Vicious

Anakin Skywalker was a remarkable young man. He was discovered by Jedi Master Qui-Gon Jinn at the age of nine when he was a slave to a scrap-shop owner. He was believed to be "The Chosen One" spoken of in the ancient prophecies who would "bring balance to the Force." His mother claimed to have not lain with a man. He was a kind and selfless little boy, who even risked his life at the age of five to save small animals from hunters.

Anakin was freed from slavery and trained in the ways of the Jedi by Obi-Wan Kenobi.

He became known as a potential leader of the Republic and perhaps the greatest Jedi ever. He knew that his abilities surpassed those of his teacher and began to show signs of arrogance, as gifted teenagers usually do. He began to disrespect his Master and slowly passed from a strong-willed child to a weak-willed young man.

When he was old enough, Anakin went to find his mother. He eventually tracked her down, but she died in his arms after being wounded by the Sandpeople.

This traumatic event sent the powerful young man into a rage. He allowed his anger to overcome him completely. The young Anakin killed everyone present, included women and children.

This was the first real sign of a potentially vicious man who might go to the Dark Side.

In other battles, Anakin allowed his rage to take control. He would repent and resolve never to let his anger control him again. This resolve, however, did not last. Time and time again, Anakin would give in to his passions.

Chancellor Palpatine, the evil one who would become emperor, saw this great power in Anakin and slowly turned him to the Dark Side. He told him that his emotions were "only natural" in the situation. He slowly helped Anakin free himself from all remorse. Eventually, Anakin pledged his allegiance to Palpatine and to the Dark Side. He became known as Darth Vader. For the rest of his days, Darth Vader embraced the Dark Side fully and completely. He had been set free from his interior struggle between good and evil.

*   *   *

As we said, Socrates and Darth Vader have a lot in common. Through a long journey, they both were freed from their struggle. They both have an internal order. The difference, of course, is that the virtuous is aimed toward the good, and the vicious is aimed toward evil; the virtuous craves the good, and the vicious craves the bad.

Human nature craves order. It doesn't like internal conflict. As we said, virtue is easy, but the dirty secret is that so is vice. If you don't show your kid that virtue is more rewarding than vice, he'll most likely seek comfort in vice.

If your kid seems strong in one area and weak in another—have no fear. You're not delusional. He's probably not schizophrenic or bipolar. He's just human. The trick, however, is to constantly reform one area of his life each and every day.

Our true happiness lies in virtue. Darth Vader was powerful.

He indulged in whatever he wanted. But he was not a happy man. There was, however, a glimpse of remorse when death approached and he looked into the eyes of his son, Luke Skywalker. Hope is always present. But we must compare this death to that of Socrates. After refusing to escape from prison, he willfully drank the hemlock. He was at peace. He was ready for the next voyage into the afterlife.

Ultimately, you are teaching your kid not just how to live but also how to die.

Chapter Four: *Playlist*

- ▸ Weak-Willed King David
  - ▷ Passions overcome reason.

- ▸ Strong-Willed Frodo
  - ▷ Reason overcomes passions.

- ▸ Socrates: A Virtuous Man is Hard to Find
  - ▷ Reason and passion both desire the good.

- ▸ Darth Vader: The Vicious
  - ▷ Reason and passion both desire evil.

— CHAPTER FIVE —

If It Ain't Easy, It Ain't Virtue

"GOOD HABITS FORMED AT YOUTH
MAKE ALL THE DIFFERENCE."
—ARISTOTLE

The Super Athletes in Mexico's Canyons

DEEP IN the deadly Copper Canyons of Mexico reside a primitive tribe of Indians. They were first discovered in the sixteenth century and haven't changed much. Outsiders call them the Tarahumara Indians. But they call themselves the Rarámuri, meaning "runners on foot" or "those who run fast." It's the perfect name for these superathletes.

Local legend spoke of natives who chase down deer and run for days without stop. These rumors traveled the world, finding their way to Christopher McDougall, a sportswriter for *Men's Health*.

McDougall was a frustrated recreational runner. Plagued with typical running injuries, he wondered how tribal people could run barefoot for countless miles without the typical runner's injuries. He traveled to Copper Canyon to find his answer. He then wrote *Born to Run* and changed forever the sport of running.

McDougall might be surprised to see why Aristotle would love his book.

"The key secret hit me like a thunderbolt," McDougall said in an interview. "It was so simple, yet such a jolt. It was this: everything I'd been taught about running was wrong. We treat running in the modern world the same way we treat childbirth—it's going to hurt, and requires special exercises and equipment, and the best you can hope for is to get it over quickly with minimal damage."

McDougall says the same thing about our perception of running as Aristotle says about our perception of virtue. We perceive virtue as a "duty" that must be done, no matter how bad it hurts. We *absolutely* have duties toward our God, family, work, and community. Many parents have forgotten this. But Aristotle sees duty as a stepping-stone to something much greater. When your kid learns to read, she frustratingly does so out of duty. But as time goes on, it becomes easier and enjoyable. What was once a duty becomes enjoyable. And so it is with virtue.

McDougall says that most people run as a means to an end: to lose weight, perform better on the athletic field, handle stress, and so on. Running has become a chore, a necessary evil. And we wonder, "Why are Americans so bad at running, and why do we get hurt so frequently?"

McDougall asked this question and found his answer: "I meet the Tarahumara, and they're having a blast. They remember what it's like to love running, and it lets them blaze through the canyons like dolphins rocketing through waves. For them, running isn't work. It isn't a punishment for eating. It's fine art, like it was for our ancestors."

Whether we are running, playing music, leading a business, or reading a book, our human nature is the same. If we embrace the "best" reason to act rather than the "right" reason (such as duty), things become easier. If your kid gets As in school because you pay him, that's good! But it is *best* for your kid to get good grades out of a love of learning. Don't let your kid settle for the second-best reason to do something. Aim for the best reason.

"The Tarahumara have a saying," McDougall continues. "'Children run before they can walk.' Watch any four-year-old— they do everything at full speed, and it's all about fun. That's the most important thing I picked up from my time in the Copper Canyons, the understanding that running can be fast and fun and spontaneous, and when it is, you feel like you can go forever."

Just like the Tarahumara Indians enjoy running, Aristotle wants your kid to enjoy virtue. Imagine if we acted only out of duty and obligation, and imagine if we communicated this to our loved ones. A wife might not be too impressed with her husband's sense of duty, as the following story shows.

* * *

Imagine a man comes home from a business trip. He walks in the door, and his wife greets him with a kiss.

"I missed you, honey," the wife says. "How was your trip?"

"It was very difficult. I am completely exhausted," he responds.

"Oh, I'm sorry," the wife answers sympathetically. "What was so difficult?"

"The difficulty was in staying faithful," her husband answers.

"Faithful to what, *dear*?" the wife demands.

"Well, faithful to you, of course," he says, surprised at her tone of voice. "Haven't you seen Victoria, my new colleague? She is a walking billboard of temptation."

By this time, the wife is staring at her idiot husband with rage in her eyes. "My dearest wife, calm down. I didn't give in. Not once! I struggled. I even prayed. I looked at your picture in my wallet. And I fought the temptation. I won! *We won*!"

The wife hits him and screams, "Get out of my house, you pervert!"

Idiot husband can't figure out what went wrong.

* * *

Many philosophers, however, would call the idiot husband "virtuous." They hold that true virtue is found in the struggle. The leading philosopher in this school of thought was Immanuel Kant, the most influential philosopher in modern times.

Kant believed that duty—as opposed to striving for happiness—was the key ingredient to the virtuous life. Living the virtuous life, for Kant, means doing one's duty without any ulterior motive. You are faithful to your wife because all men *should be* faithful to their wives. You give money to charity because all men *should be* charitable. You play ball with your kids because all fathers *should* play ball with their kids. Desiring one's wife, having a charitable heart, or enjoying playtime with your kids is irrelevant for Kant.

Aristotle believed that a man who desired none other than his wife was more virtuous because more "of himself" was involved: his reason and his passions. Desiring a good thing is far more important than merely doing it.

Do not let any of this negate the importance of duties. Modern parents seem to have forgotten all about them. Your kid has duties to God, family, work, community, and even the little things. If your kid does not learn to abide by his duties of making his bed, doing his homework, saying "yes sir," and so on, he will not learn to enjoy the goodness that comes from good action.

Aristotle would remind you, however, that performing one's duty is not equivalent to being virtuous. Performing a duty can in fact be a morally neutral event. Consider the following three scenarios:

Scenario 1: Your kid can make his bed because he has been told to.

Scenario 2: Your kid can make his bed because he is beginning to see the value of taking care of his things.

Scenario 3: Your kid can make his bed because he is trying to hide something under the covers.

In all three scenarios, your kid fulfilled his duty. There is nothing wrong with scenario 1: kids have to start somewhere. You want him ultimately to learn the value in scenario 2, which is the best of the three scenarios. Scenario 3 is not only *not* good, but it's bad. Forget the "duty" to make his bed. He is being dishonest. And worse, he makes it appear he has done a good thing when in fact he's done the opposite.

To understand better the difference between Immanuel Kant and Aristotle, think of it this way: Kant would have no interest in the Tarahumara Indians, but Aristotle would. Aristotle would see this race of people as a great example of how human beings (your kid included) can enjoy the virtuous life. Virtue, for Aristotle, is something that becomes easy precisely because you end up doing what you love. The Tarahumara people love to run, which makes them the best runners in the world. Holy men and women love to be virtuous, which makes them the best people in the world.

Raising kids is all about showing them *how* to live and *why* to live that way. And the greatest attribute of virtue is that it is the most rewarding thing to do.

So, what is virtue? We know it's more than duty and we know it's supposed to be easy. But what *is* it? Let's break down Aristotle's definition.

Virtue Is a Habit: You Are What You Eat

> "Virtue is **a habit** . . ."

There are not only bad habits. There are good habits. They make things easy.

Think of the good habits your kid may possess. Do these make her less virtuous? When good habits go on autopilot, you know your kid has come a long way.

Verbal Habits: "Please," "Thank you," "Yes Sir." These should be on autopilot. The older the kid, the harder it is to form this habit. Start young!

Physical Habits: Standing up straight, sitting like a lady, making eye contact. The more habitual, the better. Who wants to think about standing up straight for the rest of her life?

Moral Habits: Aristotle lists a ton of them, many of which we'll discuss later. Moral habits include prudence, justice, courage, and temperance. Once courage, for example, becomes "second nature" to your kids, they will face any circumstance with the same courageous character.

We've all heard the saying "You are what you eat." This is very Aristotelian. When you form a habit, it becomes a part of you. You become what you do. One action is not a habit, nor is it a virtue. If your kid is generally rude, but says "please" out of the blue, he's still a "rude kid." If he works at it and begins saying "please" some of the time, he becomes a quasi-polite kid. Eventually, good manners will begin rolling off his tongue. You now have a polite kid.

Notice the process: he was initially *weak-willed*, then through repetition, he became *strong-willed*, and through more repetition, he became *virtuous*. He *became* something else; he became a polite kid. This is radically different from being a rude kid that says a polite word. For Aristotle, this is a huge difference.

Virtue is much like running cross-country or swimming: you can't think your way to the finish life. You must act your way to virtue. In short, one good act is not good enough for cross-country, for swimming, for playing an instrument, and it certainly isn't enough for virtue. Without habits, your kid is simply doing random acts, sometimes good, sometimes bad. He deserves more.

Chosen for Its Own Sake

> "Virtue is a habit **of choosing** . . ."

Choosing to do good means choosing good *for its own sake*. Let's consider your kid's choice to say please. Let's say "please" is now a habit. But what if it is a habit *only* because you gave him a dime every time he said "please"? Is he saying "please" for *virtue's own sake*? No, he isn't. He's saying please for money. This is fine in the beginning, but Aristotle would say virtue is still not present.

Let's take a more serious example. Assume your teenager wants to be the best athlete possible. He goes to the gym. He works hard. He eats healthy. Many of these traits are becoming habitual. He appears to be temperate.

What if you found out he was doing all this for the sole purpose of getting a girl into bed! The varsity players get all the girls! This isn't unnatural. If he isn't trying to impress girls, something might be wrong. But in this case, the virtue of temperance is not being done *for its own sake*. Aristotle says, "Sorry, but not a virtue."

How many adults develop certain skill sets for bad motives,

such as fame or fortune? This cannot be overlooked. Far too often, pride is the driving force behind an adult's apparent temperance. How many people who go to church weekly are going simply as a public sign of their own sanctity? How many people give grand donations as a public witness to their magnanimity? Choosing to do good for *its own sake* is sorely overlooked, but not by Aristotle.

Additionally, an accident is not choosing. Assume you tell your kid to put away the milk. A few minutes later you go to get it and find it on the counter. Far too often, the parent's response is, "Ah, perfect. I needed it anyway." Obviously, your kid did not do the right thing. It just ended up OK for you. This is called being a utilitarian. People far too often judge things by the practical use to them. We'll talk more about utilitarians later.

It's part of our human nature to look for the bright side of a situation. We say things like "No harm, no foul," or "All's well that ends well." As an adult, you and I have grown far too comfortable with these clichés. As long as we get what we want, we'll overlook the way in which we got there. But don't do this with your kids. Your kid must choose virtue *for its own sake.* Happiness does not happen by mistake.

The Mean between Extremes

"Virtue is a habit of choosing the **mean between extremes . . .**"

You probably know the story of Icarus. Icarus and his father, Daedalus, were trapped on the island of Crete. So Daedalus crafted wings of feathers and wax so Icarus could fly from the island. Before Icarus took flight, Daedalus warned him not to fly too close to the sun or too close to the water.

Icarus, however, didn't listen and flew too high. The wax that held the wings together melted in the heat of the sun, and Icarus plunged into the sea and drowned.

The story of Icarus is often interpreted as a moral lesson on hubris or "flying too high." And it is. But it's about more than that. Daedalus also warned Icarus not to fly too low, to stay away from the cresting sea.

The ancients, particularly Aristotle, had a keen understanding of *moderation*. Aristotle coined the phrase "Virtue stands in the middle between extremes."

— THE GOLDEN MEAN THROUGH HISTORY —

Cicero: "Never go to excess, but let moderation be your guide."

Epictetus: "If one oversteps the bounds of moderation, the greatest pleasures cease to please."

William Shakespeare: "They are sick that surfeit with too much, as they that starve with nothing."

Hindu Proverb: "Even nectar is poison if taken to excess."

Confucius: "To go beyond is as wrong as to fall short."

Tony to Angela on *Who's the Boss*: "You're always in either first or fifth, but you know, there's a lot of great gears in between."

Icarus was told not to fly too close to the sun or the water. Virtue avoids both extremes, not just one. Aristotle said that every virtue has two corresponding vices, one on each extreme.

Aristotle provides a few examples of virtues and their extremes.

The Virtue of Courage

COWARDICE   **COURAGE**   RASHNESS

Aristotle says, "The man who faces and who fears the right things and from the right motive, in the right way and at the right time, and who feels confidence under the corresponding conditions, is brave."

Courage is the "mean" between fear and rashness. You've probably experienced both with your kids. One day they are too afraid to take the training wheels off; the next they're Rollerblading through a busy intersection. Aristotle says, "A man is not a coward if he fears insult to his wife and children or envy or anything of the kind; nor brave if he is confident when he is about to be flogged." It is good to fear some things. It's good for a brother to fear his sister's being the butt of a joke, and for a sister to fear her brother's getting beat up by bullies.

The Virtue of Temperance

INSENSIBILITY   **TEMPERANCE**   SELF-INDULGENCE

Aristotle understood children very well. He equated the self-indulgent man to a child, "since children in fact live at the beck and call of appetite, and it is in them that the desire for what is pleasant is strongest."

Aristotle gives the self-indulgent a great name: Belly-Gods. He would conclude that modern kids (and parents) worship their bellies. As a culture, we have lost almost all ability to exercise self-control. One simple way to overcome this is simply to eat healthy.

On the other extreme of temperance is insensibility. "People who fall short with regard to pleasure, and delight in them less than they should, are hardly found; for such insensibility is not human." Don't take away your kid's pleasures; just encourage the right kind in the right amount.

The Virtue of Generosity

GREEDINESS   **GENEROSITY**   WASTEFULNESS

Here we mean generosity in terms of wealth, whether that be money or other possessions. Kids, of course, don't really have money, but they can share their toys or give things to the poor. "Mine!" is a bad word, and it's one of the first words a kid will say.

My house is a magnet for other people's stuff. Because we have so many kids, people give us their hand-me-downs. The kids get new clothes and toys all the time—too often, in fact. So, every few months we clean out their rooms and give some things to the poor. It takes them about thirty seconds to get over it. As it turns out, they enjoy it most of the time.

In the end, it allows them to 1) focus on the toys they still have, 2) get pleasure from being generous to the poor, and 3) keep them from getting too attached to any material thing.

On one extreme, you have stingy or greedy people. This is Ebenezer Scrooge. Kids have this tendency but can easily be led away from this vice. Greed is one of the most insidious vices: it's a black hole that sucks in all of your possessions and happiness. Greedy people are the unhappiest people in the world, just like Scrooge before his conversion.

On the other extreme, you have wasteful or extravagant people. This might manifest itself as flashy or gaudy as an adult, showing off the new outfit or embroidered table napkins. (It's amazing how silly adults can be.) It's fine for a kid to be proud of his new shoes, but he can take it too far. He can begin judging others based on their shoes. Girls are the worst at this. Aristotle would say that moderation in possession and donation to the poor are the ways to avoid this extreme.

Mentors: Aristotle's Support for Parental Outsourcing

> "Virtue is a habit of choosing the mean between extremes **according to the right reason of a wise person.**"

You are the primary teacher for your kids. You are their model. The reality, however, is that you aren't the model of every virtue.

You need help from the experts (and I don't mean "child experts"). Find a person who is virtuous in the area of concern, and seek his guidance. Most moral situations are beset with personal circumstances and exterior pressures that factor heavily into one's discernment. Aristotle knows that it is far too difficult for a person to wade through these situations alone, so he tells us to find a mentor for our particular situation.

For example, if your kid is discerning how to handle a bully at school, maybe mom and dad are poor role models. Maybe they are too timid, or simply never had to deal with bullies. Or perhaps they are too aggressive to give good advice. How about other adults? Maybe the gym coach, or grandpa, or an aunt or uncle. It is your responsibility to find the right doctor based on the illness, and the right teacher based on the area of study. Likewise, it is your responsibility to find the right mentor based on the virtue at hand.

You could never supply all your kid's medical or education needs. You cannot provide all his moral needs either.

There is a process to follow in finding the right person. First, you must determine the moral issue at hand. Does the situation require courage, like standing up to a bully? Does the situation require prudence, like helping your kid discern which college to attend? Does the situation require generosity, like helping your kid to be nice to the nerds at school? Does the situation require purity, like helping your teenager figure out how to date honorably?

Aristotle would recommend that you make a list of the people you know who possess different virtues. Who do you know who deals well with particular situations? Putting pen to paper will bring much of this to the forefront of your mind.

After determining the virtuous people in your life, Aristotle would have you *observe them*, not just talk with them. Sometimes the people best at something can't explain it very well. They just do it. Virtue is often the same way.

Even if these people can't explain themselves very well, they can still be mentors for your kid. Their actions speak louder than words. Therefore, be sure to help your kid understand that example is the greatest teacher of all.

The Complete Definition of Virtue

> **"Virtue is a habit of choosing the mean between extremes in accordance with the right reasoning of a wise person."**

This looks like a mouthful, but we have broken it down piece by piece and now understand it in its entirety. Here's a quick summary of each part:

Virtue is:

1. **"a habit":** Habits make things easy. Not all habits are bad. Practice makes perfect, and practice makes things easy. The struggle between reason and passion is the beginning of development, not the end. We are made for more than struggle.

2. **"of choosing":** Choosing is an intentional act. Don't think that habit eliminates choice. It doesn't. Furthermore, we must choose a good *for its own sake*, not for an ulterior motive. Pay attention to your kid's motives and direct his motives. The act itself is only half the battle.

3. **"the mean between extremes":** Moderation is the key. Every virtue has two extreme vices. Identify the moral dilemma at hand and then identify the extremes on both sides of the virtue. The extremes are easier to see than the mean, so it helps to start with the extremes. Help him navigate through the middle.

4. **"in accordance with the right reasoning of a wise person":** YOU aren't the wisest, holiest, most prudent person in the world. Find virtuous people in your life. Get your kid to watch the way they live. Actions are louder than words.

These are the elements of Aristotle's definition of virtue. It's a beautiful thing. Each part of the definition is easy to understand.

Being a parent is risky business. You can give it your all, and your kid can break your heart. The most heartbreaking thing, however, should not be that your kid turns his back on you, but on virtue. Your kid can live a happy life without you, but not without virtue.

But virtue isn't enough. Your kid is not just a rational animal. He's a social animal as well.

During this journey toward virtue, your kid will go far beyond you. He will be influenced by many other people. And this is why

Aristotle said that humans are not only rational animals but also "social" animals.

As a parent, you must come to terms with a cold, hard fact: you will not always be the most important person in your kid's life. Your kid, however, will always have important people in his life. The question is who. Who will be the significant other? Who will be his best friend? Who will he marry? These relationships will, hopefully, outlive mom and dad.

Your kid is a social animal who needs a "pack." But this is risky business. Therefore, in part II we'll look at your kid's social nature. We'll talk about Nazis and how they did what they did. We'll talk about dating. We'll talk about Facebook "friends." Ultimately, we'll talk about how true friendship is necessary for your kid to obtain true happiness.

Chapter Five: *Playlist*

- ▶ Remember the Tarahumara Indians: Running has become easy. And so can virtue become easy.

- ▶ The definition of virtue:
  - ▷ Virtue is a habit.
  - ▷ Virtue is chosen for its own sake.
  - ▷ Virtue is the mean between extremes.
  - ▷ Virtue is in accordance with the right reasoning of a wise person.

- ▶ You're not perfect! Find mentors for your kids. Outsource some of your parenting.
  - ▷ Virtue isn't enough.

— Part II —

Friendship

"Friendship is a single soul dwelling in two bodies."

—Aristotle

CHAPTER SIX

Your Kid Is a Social Animal

"MAN, WHEN PERFECTED, IS THE BEST OF
ANIMALS, BUT WHEN SEPARATED FROM LAW
AND JUSTICE, HE IS THE WORST OF ALL."
—ARISTOTLE

HOW COULD average Nazi soldiers break apart families, starve innocent people, lead countless human beings to the gas chambers, and participate in lethal medical experiments on children? Was every Nazi as evil as Hitler?

More important: How would *we* have acted in their situations? Would our friends, neighbors, loved ones, and children have had the moral courage to resist? Or is there a potential Nazi inside all of us?

We are so certain that such acts are beyond our ability. We are so certain that we are truly incapable of such atrocities and that we would prefer to die than partake in such evil. But how certain are you? Are you certain your own child would have the moral strength to walk away from such a situation?

These questions prompted Yale psychologist Dr. Stanley

Milgram to perform an eye-opening experiment. Milgram proved that people like you and me can become something beyond our own comprehension within minutes of entering a classic obedience/authority scenario.

The Milgrim Experiment

Milgrim's experiment began in July 1961, one year after the trial of Adolf Eichmann, the notorious Nazi officer who sent countless people to their death. During his trial in Jerusalem, Eichmann defended himself, as did those who were tried at Nuremburg following World War II.

"I was following orders," said Eichmann. "I never did anything, great or small, without obtaining in advance express instructions from Adolf Hitler or any of my superiors." It was this defense that caused Milgram to undertake his experiment, to examine how difficult it is to get others to cooperate with evil acts.

Milgram's experiments involved testing volunteers for their willingness to administer electric shocks to innocent strangers. The volunteers were recruited from newspaper ads asking for participants in a study of how people learn. In return they were paid $4.50 per hour.

The recruits were told to read questions to test subjects who sat behind a wall and were hooked up to electrical wires. If the subject got the question wrong, the questioner was to administer a shock. The more questions the subject got wrong, the stronger the voltage.

The recruits, upon hearing the subjects scream in pain, often pleaded to be let out of the test. They asked the doctor to end the experiment. They protested that it wasn't fair. They got up to leave. They showed great signs of remorse. But a single man, an authority figure dressed in a white coat, would simply say, "Please sit down and read the next question. The test must go on." The questioner would say, "I don't want responsibility for this man getting hurt." "It is my responsibility," the doctor would reply.

And amazingly, the recruits would stay. The recruits would repeatedly violate their conscience and continue to shock the subject, even to apparent death.

In reality, the subject was an actor. He received no shock at all. But America was shocked. In Milgram's experiment, the average person did exactly what Nazi soldiers did, what Eichmann claimed to have done in his Jerusalem trial: he carried out the commands of an authority figure, regardless of the promptings of his own conscience.

The Stanford Experiment

Ten years after Milgrim's experiments at Yale, an even more shocking experiment at Stanford University showed how powerfully our social environment can form—and deform—our self-identity.

In the summer of 1971, Dr. Phillip Zimbardo, professor of psychology at Stanford, embarked on an experiment funded by the U.S. military to examine the causes of conflict between guards and prisoners.

In the basement of Stanford's psychology building, Zimbardo created a mock prison. From August 14 to August 20, 1971, volunteer college students agreed to play the role of either military guard or prisoner for a stipend of fifteen dollars a day.

Zimbardo divided the participants into twenty-four guards and fifty-one inmates. The "prisoners" had their mug shots taken and were fingerprinted by Palo Alto police before being transported to the "prison" in the basement of Jordan Hall, Stanford's psychology building.

The prisoners were strip-searched and dressed in typical inmate attire. They were referred to only by their inmate numbers. For as long as they chose to participate in the experiment, they were forbidden to leave.

The guards were outfitted in the style of actual jail guards, complete with dark sunglasses and wooden batons. They worked in eight-hour shifts and could leave the premises when they went off duty.

It was all very authentic . . . and the results were all too real.

From the beginning, at the strip search, the guards degraded the prisoners, mocking their genitals. By the second day, things were worse. The prisoners, led by inmate #8612, barricaded their cell. The guards removed #8612 and placed him in solitary confinement, after which the other prisoners began cursing the guards. The guards responded by waking up the prisoners at all hours, forcing them to perform exhausting exercises and to scrub toilets with their bare hands.

Finally, #8612 asked to be let out of the experiment. Dr. Zimbardo, acting as prison superintendant, instead offered him a deal: become an informant.

Prisoner #8612 went back to the cell and told the others they weren't allowed to leave. He began acting crazy: shouting, cursing, thrashing about. The other prisoners became even more afraid, though #8612 was then dismissed from the experiment. Reality and make believe were becoming indistinguishable.

Rumors spread that #8612 was going to return with reinforcements to liberate the prisoners. Zimbardo (by this point, fully immersed in his own experiment) tore down the prison and moved the inmates to another part of the school. When no jailbreak occurred, the guards were instructed to rebuild the prison. They weren't happy with this extra work.

Some of the guards began taking out their frustration on the prisoners, verbally abusing them, placing them in solitary confinement, and stripping them of their blankets and mattresses.

Prisoner #819 barricaded himself and finally asked to leave, but the remaining prisoners began chanting, "Eight-nineteen did a bad thing! Eight-nineteen did a bad thing! Eight-nineteen did a bad thing!" The prisoner became upset that he couldn't leave, when Zimbardo reminded him that it was just an experiment. So 819 left and was replaced by 416, who immediately went on a hunger strike. He was put in solitary and verbally abused by the guards and the prisoners.

The most notorious guard, nicknamed John Wayne, decided to conduct his own experiment, offering to let 416 out of solitary if all the other prisoners gave up their blankets for a night. The prisoners refused.

On day 6, Zimbardo's girlfriend and future wife, a graduate student at Stanford, came to visit. She was shocked at the behavior of all involved and at the conditions in which the prisoners were living. Her shock snapped Zimbardo out of his own role-playing. He cut short the experiment, which had been scheduled to run two weeks.

The experiment had gone horribly wrong. But there were some interesting conclusions to be drawn.

For instance, the prisoners, free to leave the experiment at any time, for the most part stayed, despite the confinement and degradation. In a sense, they had *become* prisoners.

As for the guards, the majority were not malicious, but even the good guards did not intervene when they saw their fellow guards being abusive and degrading.

*   *   *

The Stanford Experiment is one of the most revealing—and terrifying—experiments in American history. But Aristotle was onto its findings a few thousand years ago.

Aristotle identified human beings as "rational animals," but he also called us *zoon politicon*, or "political animals." "Political" because Aristotle really means "social." We are social animals, animals created to live in community. Our human nature requires that we seek out relationships and develop through interaction with others.

— MORE ON THE STANFORD EXPERIMENT —

Dr. Zimbardo runs a website (www.prisonexp.org) with information and video on his infamous experiment. The site also features incisive discussion questions. Here are some to get you going:

▸ If you were a guard, what type of guard would you have become? How sure are you?

▸ What is identity? Is there a core to your self-identity independent of how others define you? How difficult would it be to remake any given person into someone with a new identity?

▸ Do you think that kids from an urban working-class environment would have broken down emotionally in the way our middle-class prisoners did? Why? What about women?

▸ After the study, how do you think the prisoners and guards felt when they saw each other in civilian clothes again and their prison reconverted to a basement laboratory hallway?

▸ Was it ethical to do this study? Was it right to trade the suffering experienced by participants for the knowledge gained by the research?

There is no Aristotelian hermit. We are made to live with others, for better—or for worse.

Aristotle says our nature is hardwired, so we respond to our social environment. Sensitivity to social cues is how your kid makes friends, how he learns to laugh at a joke, how he learns to blend in.

And these are good traits to have. "Fitting in" isn't bad per se. In most circumstances, the old adage "When in Rome, do as the Romans" holds true.

Man has an innate desire for community, for unity with others. Adapting to our environment and "fitting in" helps us achieve community. Yes, social interaction and responding to our environment is important, but the Stanford Experiment shows that all social interactions and adaptations are not created equal. What would this experiment represent to Aristotle?

Just as there is nothing wrong with our passions, there is nothing wrong with adapting to our environment. Passions are good or at least neutral in themselves, problems arise only when they are directed to bad things. Likewise, our ability to influence and be influenced by others is a simple reality of our human nature, good in itself. But problems arise when this ability to influence is used for evil.

In the Stanford Experiment, young, healthy, smart, well-adjusted college students were severely altered by their environment, to the point of nearly forgetting their real identity. Afterward, the John Wayne guard admitted, "You really become that person once you put on that khaki uniform, you put on the glasses, you take the night stick." But it wasn't just the costume; it was the entire social environment that changed him. He had gotten other guards to join him in doling out abuse. The students playacting as prisoners became like actual prisoners to the guards. The more the prisoners became prisoners, the more the guards became guards. As the prisoners began to beg to be let out of the experiment, the guards became emboldened. They felt their power increase as they watched the prisoners grow weaker.

The reverse was true as well. Some of the prisoners became prisoners in their own mind. Prisoner 819 wanted to leave but refused because he had angered the other prisoners. Zimardo had to remind him that it was just an experiment. When the guards offered to let a fellow student out of solitary confinement if his peers gave up their blankets, the prisoners refused. They began to self-identity as prisoners rather than as college students participating in an experiment. And Dr. Zimbardo? He began to self-identify as the prison supervisor.

Aristotle would say, yes, your kid *could* be one of those guards in the Stanford Experiment. He *could* be one of the prisoners, fighting for nothing but self-preservation and small comforts. Or, like the volunteers in the Milgrim Experiment, he *could* administer electric shocks to strangers.

None of us are immune to the influences of our social environment. But forewarned is, to some extent, forearmed. Aristotle would say it is vital that you give your kid a clear understanding of social interaction—of how others influence him, and how he influences others too.

As a social animal, your kid is heavily influenced by people's words, actions, and even body language. Our sensitivity to social influences is deeply ingrained in our nature, observable even shortly after birth, as another famous experiment shows.

The Still Face Experiment

Dr. Amanda Jones of Warwick Medical School works with at-risk families. "The Still Face Experiment," she says, "is a wonderful experiment because primarily it shows you the sensitivity a baby has to loss, and to loss of contact with, if the relationship is developing well, a very loved figure."

Leila is a happy one-year-old. She is playing with her mom, Amy. Leila is sitting in her high chair, smiling and laughing as she and her mom pass a stuffed animal back and forth. Amy shows

Leila a little doggy, and Leila begins to touch it. She is happy and engaged.

Then Dr. Jones knocks on the two-way mirror behind which she's been observing the interaction. Amy, on cue, stops everything and gives Leila a still face: nothing but a stare. Not a mean look; just a bland, expressionless stare.

Leila is not happy with the change. She stares back as if saying, what is wrong? Within seconds, she becomes upset and begins to cry. And this is good. "It would be very alarming," says Dr. Jones, "if a baby was not disturbed by the still face, if it seemed the norm. That would be disturbing."

Then mommy engages again. Within moments the baby has forgiven mommy. She brightens up and smiles once more. "There has been a rupture, but then they were repaired and got back on track," says Dr. Jones. "You could say that mom was forgiven, quite quickly. Whereas if the baby stays inconsolable, and can't get back on track, that would also be very important information."

*   *   *

The babies in the Still Face Experiment prove Aristotle right in asserting that humans have an innate need for social interaction. Babies, at least those living in a happy home, expect mommy to smile and look at them and engage in baby talk. In other words, babies have already learned something about what it means to love. And when that love, that type of social interaction, is removed, they react strongly, revolting against the antisocial behavior of mommy.

The babies' reaction to the Still Face is more than a frustration with being ignored. A busy mommy is forced to ignore her baby all the time: the phone rings, the other kids need something, she has to get her work done. No mom or dad can engage with their baby 100 percent of the time.

But in the Still Face Experiment, the mommy doesn't turn her attention from baby to something else. She continues to look at baby, but expressionlessly, with a blank stare. And the baby instinctively responds to this lack of expression with distress, greater even than if mommy were angry or sad. Disengagement from your child is worse than losing your temper with her or getting upset.

Anger is not the opposite of love. Even the extreme of hatred is not the opposite of love. The opposite of love is apathy.

Love is an active engagement between two people. Hate is also an active engagement but with an entirely different objective. Apathy, however, is no activity and no engagement.

Aristotle would be interested in the Still Face Experiment because it shows that an apathetic face is completely antithetical to our human nature. It's as if the baby were screaming out, "I am a social creature! Engage! Engage! Whatever you do, just don't give me that blank face!" In short, the Still Face Experiment is evidence of a child's innate desire for human interaction.

Our next experiment shows the consequences of negative interaction. The Milgrim and Stanford Experiments show the powerful influence the social environment has on an adult. But just how long does it take to make an impact on a kid? The Bobo Doll Experiment provides the answer, albeit in a distressing way.

The Bobo Doll Experiment

In 1961 and 1963, Albert Bandura, a psychologist at Stanford, conducted a set of experiments to observe how children react to the behavior of adults. Bandura put an adult and a child into a room together. The child was told that a certain set of toys was only for the adult to play with. This set of toys included a mallet and a Bobo doll. In some cases, the adult would beat and kick and yell aggressively at the Bobo doll for a few minutes.

Then the adult would be taken out of the room, and the child would be allowed to play with the toys. In cases where a child had watched the adult act aggressively, the child acted more aggressively. When the sexes were the same—that is, when a boy watched a man, and a girl watched a women—the level of aggression was even higher.

As a parent, you could have guessed this. Have you ever lost your temper in front of your kid? Of course you have. Did you notice whether your kid began mimicking you within minutes? Your kids learn how to act from their social environment. And they learn quickly.

Time and time again, we find scientists from all branches of study going to great lengths to prove basic principles of human nature. It's nice to see that scientists have figured out that kids learn how to act from watching adults. But they really didn't need a mallet and Bobo doll. All they had to do was consult Aristotle.

Your Kid's Social Environment . . . Is You

As a parent, the Still Face and Bobo Doll Experiments should reinforce the old saying "You never get a second chance to make a first impression."

As a parent, you are your kid's first impression of people, of the world, of the universe—of reality itself. Your kid knows that you exist before she knows that she exists herself. Yours is the first face she learns to love. And oddly enough, she'll love you even if you are a pretty terrible parent.

Children are forgiving creatures, but they're also impressionable. As a parent, you embody all that is good and all that is bad in their world because you *are* their whole world. Babies have no knowledge of anything other than their mother's voice and their mother's touch. Make sure it is a good one.

In every decision you make as a parent, you must consider the social aspects of your kid's nature. It will help to shape his daily life, his education, his religious development—everything in your kid's life is dependent on his social nature. You can't remove his social nature any more than you can remove his rationality or his passions. Rather, you should embrace it and aim to develop in your child a true and abiding sense of community and friendship.

In part I, we discussed how your kid is a rational animal. He's also a social animal, and the key component to understanding what Aristotle means by calling your kid a "social animal" is to dive deep into his philosophy of friendship.

This is what we'll explore in the next chapter. Suffice it to say . . . it is probably NOT what you think.

Chapter Six: *Playlist*

▸ The *Milgram Experiment* "shockingly" shows that the average person will carry out the commands of an authority figure, regardless of what his own conscience says.

▸ The *Stanford Experiment* shows we not only listen to authority but can also take on whatever persona the environment demands.

▸ The *Still Face Experiment* proves that humans, even babies, have an innate need for social interaction.

▸ The *Bobo Doll Experiment* proves how quickly your kid will be influenced by *you*!

CHAPTER SEVEN

The Three Types of Friendship

"MY BEST FRIEND IS THE MAN WHO
IN WISHING ME WELL WISHES IT
FOR MY OWN SAKE."

—ARISTOTLE

"WITHOUT FRIENDS no one would choose to live, even though he had all other goods." That's how Aristotle begins his treatment on friendships in *Nicomachean Ethics*. It's a nice saying, but is it true? Are friends better than money? A big house? A Corvette?

For Aristotle, the mansion, the fast car, the bags of money, are good, but they're nothing compared with true friendship. That's why lottery winners commit suicide, and celebrities and rock stars keep chasing the next high. They have all the money in the world. But it's not enough.

There are many different uses of the term *friend*, and while most of them aren't wrong, they aren't exactly accurate. Often we refer to someone as a "good friend" when really they're just a "good acquaintance." For your kids, they might be a "good playmate" or a "good study partner."

You've probably begun to wonder what sort of "friends" your kid has. Sometimes you might not like the kid next door, but he is an acceptable playmate. You hope your kid doesn't develop a real attachment, but the neighbor kid isn't so bad as to kick him out of your backyard. Or what about your kid's basketball teammates? They're fine for sports, but maybe you don't want your kid spending too much time with them off the court.

You might scratch your head at this point and wonder, "Is my kid 'friends' with these other kids?" Aristotle would say, yes . . . on some level.

Aristotle says there are three different types of friendship:

1. Useful Friendships
2. Pleasure Friendships
3. True Friendships

All three types are real friendships, but their objectives vary greatly. Aristotle thus provides a very broad definition for friendship in general and then places the three different types within it.

According to Aristotle, ***Friendship is the mutual recognition of wishing well between two people.*** Let's break this down.

Wishing Well

The most fundamental element of friendship is wishing the other well. If your motives are purely selfish, then there is no friendship. Wishing well refers to wanting a good for someone else. When a mechanic fixes your car, you want the best deal you can get, but you also want him to make out well. You will haggle him down, you might shop around for the best price, but you have no intent of hurting him. In fact, you genuinely want a "win / win."

Between Two People

Aristotle calls this "reciprocity." In other words, it takes two to tango. Both parties involved must want the "win/win." If you wish your mechanic well, but he's trying to rip you off, there's no friendship.

Mutually Recognized

Finally, the goodwill between the two people must also be *mutually recognized.* Both you and your mechanic have to know that each of you is wishing the other well. Mutually recognizing these two good things (each of your good wills) gives life to a third good, friendship. This is a beautiful thing—even with your mechanic.

If there is a "mutual recognition of wishing well between two people," there is friendship in a general sense. So you and your mechanic are indeed friends. And this is good. It's just not a "true" friendship.

Useful Friendships: Utilitarians in the Sandbox

According to Aristotle's definition, you *are* friends with your mechanic. Not to mention your doctor and your employer. What about your kid? Is he "friends" with his teacher or study partners? How about his coach? Aristotle would say, "Yes, sort of."

You and your mechanic have a useful friendship, rooted in the mutual benefits you provide each other. Your friendship is not rooted in unconditional love for each other. In fact, it's 100 percent conditional. You are friends as long as you are both seeking a certain outcome. Once that outcome is achieved, the friendship is over.

Your neighbors are often useful friends. We have all had the experience of disliking a neighbor. Nonetheless, you are "friendly." You might keep a spare key for them. They might lend a hand when a tree falls in your yard. You might commiserate when the HOA tries to raise dues again. Many little things bring you together. You wish each other well, because what is good for your neighbor is probably good for you, and your neighbor feels the same. Aristotle would say you have all the elements of a useful friendship.

Your kid has useful friendships too. Studying (and school in general) brings certain kids together who wouldn't otherwise hang out. If helping each other on an exam is mutually recognized, you have a useful friendship. Once the exam is over, the friendship terminates. Again, this is OK, so long as it is dealt with maturely and graciously.

It's important to help your kid see there is nothing wrong, per se, with useful friendships. But remember, if there is anything dishonest or deceptive or one-sided about the arrangement, it is not a friendship at all. Rather it's one person using the other.

Useful friendships are essential for getting through life, especially as one gets older. As a parent, you should know when your kid is entering into a useful friendship. Then you can help him handle it properly and not be shocked when it comes to an end.

The most important thing to remember about useful friendships is that they are imperfect. They are useful but never deeply satisfying. They never last long. And they can devolve into something truly utilitarian if you aren't careful.

A utilitarian judges things, actions, and people primarily upon their "utility." It's a very real and tempting thing, even in the sandbox. The key difference between utilitarianism and useful friendships is the mutual *wishing well* of the other. This is not *using* someone purely for your own purposes, which is far too common and very damaging.

Aristotle would warn parents to protect their children from "using" other people. There is a good and honorable way to have a useful friendship, but it is wrong to manipulate people for our own purposes. It is vitally important for you to watch for this subtle distinction in the relationships forged by your kid.

Pleasure Friendships: Epicureans in the Sandbox

In a useful friendship, each party seeks the usefulness of the other person. In a pleasure friendship, each party seeks the pleasure they receive from the other person.

In a pleasure friendship, there is mutuality in wishing that the other person enjoy him or herself. Each friend truly wishes that the other has fun. But when the fun stops, the friendship stops. There is nothing deeper holding them together.

Aristotle explains that pleasure friendships are found less often in older people, who are more concerned with cultivating useful friendships. Pleasure friendships may sound bad, but they're not. There's nothing wrong with pleasure—we are not Stoics. As a parent, it is your job to teach your kid the proper place and use of pleasure. Pleasure friendships can actually develop into true friendships. But they can also easily lead to immoral relationships.

Let's look at some examples, first with adults.

The most obvious example of pleasure friendships is found in sexual relationships. Here, two people wish that the other enjoys himself or herself. Sexual relationships also serve as good examples to show that pleasure friendships can either be moral or immoral.

Two human beings can enter into a purely carnal, sexual relationship, desiring no more than to give each other great physical pleasure so they keep coming back for more. No virtue is needed here, and in fact such relationships are deeply immoral.

But in the Aristotelian sense, each partner wishes the other partner well, and so the relationship is a "friendship." Nonetheless, Aristotle would say that seeking pleasure for its own sake leads to a life without true friendship, and thus an unhappy life. In other words, pleasure is perhaps the weakest of all glues that hold people together. It came as no surprise to Aristotle, nor should it to you, that fornication leads to loneliness and misery. In a very real sense, fornication and other sexual vices are contrary to our nature precisely because they prevent people from developing true friendships.

On the other hand, pleasure friendships, including a sexual relationships, can be part of a true friendship. Marriage is the only institution in which the pleasures of a sexual relationship can in fact enhance and deepen a true and virtuous friendship; here pleasure has found its proper home. The sexual pleasure is no longer trying to stand on its own two feet, but resides within a relationship with goodness and happiness as its only objective.

Not all pleasure friendships are so intimate, or potentially dangerous, as sexual relationships. Think of your buddies at work. We all need a reprieve from the day-to-day boredom we face at the office. Most people have a few people at work they hang out with to help pass the time. Maybe they are your regular lunch buddy, or even a smoking partner. Maybe you have a similar interest, like a favorite sports team. There are countless little things that can bring people together. There's nothing wrong with this, so long as you remember that once the common element of enjoyment goes away, so will the relationship.

— FAMOUS FRIENDSHIPS —

David and Jonathan
Mary and Elizabeth
St. John and Jesus
Teresa of Avila and John of the Cross
Frodo Baggins and Sam Gamgee
Tom Sawyer and Huckleberry Finn
Anne Shirley and Diana Barry
Butch and Sundance

Just like you, your kid desires pleasure friendships, no matter what his age. Little kids aren't capable of forging true friendships (which we will discuss later), but they can have healthy pleasure friendships.

As we've seen, your kid is a social animal. She is extremely sensitive to her surrounding environment and very impressionable. And because it is natural for her to seek out pleasure friendships, you have to be extremely aware of those around her.

It's important to identify when your kid is engaged in a pleasure friendship, but beyond that, you should ask: what is the specific "pleasure" your kid is seeking in this friendship? Aristotle was the king of precision. If his child were running around Athens with a group of kids, he would think very carefully about what his kid's real motives were. Does he just want to play ball? Is he seeking the pleasure of humor? Does he enjoy being the "ring leader"? Is he trying to be one of the "cool kids"?

Aristotle drew distinctions until he was blue in the face, and we, as parents, should too. Don't settle for shrugging your shoulders and saying, "My kid is just having fun." You must determine his precise motives if at all possible.

As we discussed earlier, Stoics wouldn't be fun playmates for your kid because they repress all emotions. On the other extreme, there was a school of thought in ancient Greece called "Epicureanism," founded by Epicurus around 307 BC. He believed pleasure was the greatest good. But Epicurus wasn't a hedonist. Pleasure, he said, was found by ridding oneself of negative emotions, by living modestly, and by coming to understand the inner workings of the world. Doesn't sound too bad, does it?

But "feeling good" while "avoiding pain" won't get you—or your kid—too far down the path to virtue. It's not much of a guiding principle. Imagine being on your deathbed and leaving one final bit of wisdom for your kid. "Son, I leave you with this: no matter what, *avoid pain at all costs.*" Not very inspiring, is it? There's nothing wrong with "feeling good" and "avoiding pain," but it isn't the ultimate good in life. Your kid's life is made for more than just moderation and a lack of pain.

Epicureans boiled down friendship to simply pleasure

friendship. There was no such thing as "true friendship" for them. You don't want your kid to make the same mistake. There are a lot of closet Epicureans these days, especially in the media.

Aristotle would want you, as a parent in the modern world, to be conscious of the image of friendship displayed in the media. There is almost never a story of true friendship. If Aristotle's kid had a TV, he would be suspicious of the examples of friendship portrayed . . . and so should you. The problem with pleasure friendship is that it can distract your kid from focusing on true friendship.

True Friendship: Aristotle's Kid in the Sandbox

"Friends have all things in common," said Plato. That can't be right, can it? Surely friends have differing interests. Life would be boring otherwise. Still, true friends have "all things in common," because true friends have one overriding interest at the forefront of their minds: the other.

In useful friendships, two people seek a good that the other can help provide. In pleasure friendships, two people enjoy some activity together. Both of these friendships, however, are rooted in something other than the good of the other person. As soon as the usefulness comes to an end, so does the useful friendship. As soon as the pleasure comes to an end, so does the pleasure friendship.

In true friendship, however, the friends are regarded as good in themselves. True friendship may be the most beautiful thing in the world. It is the most real thing in the world, but it is almost other-worldly. True friendship comes from a desire to love the other person because of *who he is*, not because of what he can provide.

When you're in a true friendship, you love the other—not because of what he can do for you, not because of the pleasure he brings to you—but simply because you love who he is. Such friends will cause you different pleasures and pains. They will be of use at times and at other times not. But who they are will never change. And as true friends, you see something in them that other people do not. They are like a vault, filled with riches beyond anyone's wildest dreams. It takes time, however, to figure out the exact combination that unlocks them.

Only a true friend can discover the combination. Upon reaching this great treasure, a whole new world, a whole new way of understanding your friend, is now before your eyes. Usually there is no turning back, and no need or desire to ever turn back. You have seen a friend's true self, and you love it and only want more of it. And the only way you can repay the favor is to give your friend the combination to your own vault in return.

When both of you have reached this point, when both vaults are open and the treasures are fully available to each other, you have a true friendship. Aristotle could not have been more right when he said, "The desire for friendship comes quickly. Friendship does not."

Who would not want such a relationship with another human being? Your nature craves it. Your kid's nature craves it. And he will seek it in many different ways throughout his life, both good and bad. Although all people desire true friendship, the harsh truth is that it isn't easy to get.

According to Aristotle, there are three prerequisites for a true friendship:

1. Both people must be virtuous.
2. Both people must care more about loving rather than being loved.
3. You can only have a few true friends.

Must Be Virtuous

True friendship can exist only between virtuous people. This means that each person is focused entirely on doing good and helping the other become even better.

Furthermore, a true friend must be a positive influence, helping the other to develop further his own virtue. A true friend draws goodness from you in new, creative, and meaningful ways. True friends urge you along the virtuous path, always giving encouragement and helping you when you fall. Aristotle is not an all-or-nothing kind of guy. He understands we all have strengths and weaknesses. And therefore a true friend has certain virtues that you don't, and vice versa. You help each other.

As a parent, Aristotle would take this point very seriously in selecting his kid's friends. He would insist that you carefully examine the traits of your kid's friends. Are they a good influence? Do they draw upon your kid's good attributes, or do they draw upon his shortcomings? Parents often speak about having to "reprogram" their kids when they come back from a sleepover. There would be less reprogramming if parents were more cautious about who their kids spent time with.

Furthermore, your kid can't be a good friend to other kids if he's not developing in his own morality. "You can't give what you don't have" is an old adage of the law, and it's very true. Try to show your kid that friendship is not merely for fun. It is also about sharing the virtues that she has developed with another person.

More about Loving than Being Loved

If you want your kid to become a true friend to another, he or she must learn how to put the interest of another at the forefront of his or her mind. There's no doubt that your kid, as a human being,

86

has a tendency toward selfishness. True friendship transcends and transforms these base human desires. Selfish becomes selfless, "caring more about loving than being loved."

Your behavior in this regard will directly inform your kid's idea of friendship. Spouses, just like little kids, too often prefer to be loved rather than to love. They have their own interest at the forefront of their minds. And your kid soaks this all in. As a parent, you must always remember that actions speak louder than words. How you treat your spouse will become the definition of friendship for your kid.

True Friendship Is Infrequent

Aristotle says you can't have lots of true friends any more than you can be deeply in love with lots of people. Even a holy monk in a monastery filled with other holy monks can have only a handful of true friends. The reason is simple: you don't have the time.

It takes time to cultivate anything beautiful in this life. You don't write a book in a month (as I have painfully learned). You don't paint a picture in a day. You don't write beautiful music in one sitting. Likewise, you don't develop a true friendship at a single party. It takes time to learn about the virtues of another, to experience them in action, and to open up to them. Once you have this true friend, it takes time to keep it going. If you lose touch too often, you slip from that deep personal connection. There simply aren't enough hours in the day to cultivate numerous true friendships.

Aristotle would tell his kid to focus on developing a few true friendships rather than racking up ten thousand Facebook "friends."

Chapter Seven: *Playlist*

- Definition: Friendship is the mutual recognition of wishing well between two people.

- *Useful Friendships* are for the sake of getting things done. Think of your mechanic and accountant. Think of your kid's study partner.

- *Pleasure Friendships* are for the sake of enjoyment. Think of playmates.

- *True Friendship* is for the sake of the other person. There are three primary qualities of true friendship:
  - ▷ Both people must be virtuous.
  - ▷ Both people care more about loving than being loved.
  - ▷ It is infrequent because it takes a lot of time and attention.

CHAPTER EIGHT

If Aristotle's Kid Was on Facebook

"A FRIEND TO ALL IS A FRIEND TO NONE."
—ARISTOTLE

Facebook and Virtual Presence

IMAGINE THAT your thirteen-year-old goes to one of her first parties. She is so excited to meet numerous kids her own age. Almost everyone there is a new face. Everyone told her where they go to school, what sports they play, what their interests are, what church they go to. They all seem so friendly, and your daughter has a blast.

But as she's leaving, the mother of the girl hosting the party pulls her aside and whispers, "You know, 70 percent of the kids here tonight lied to you." Your daughter, so happy moments before, thinks, "How am I supposed to be friends with these people if from the moment we meet they are telling me lies?"

* * *

According to the Pew Internet and American Life Project, nearly 70 percent of all twelve- to fourteen-year-old kids lie on their Facebook profile. We all know that kids sometimes exaggerate, looking to give themselves a better image. It's normal. But seven kids out of ten lying on their Facebook profile is a staggering number. And it doesn't take an Aristotle to figure out why they lie so readily on the Web. There is no accountability. It's an artificial world to them.

Aristotle would not condemn Facebook or other social networking sites, but he'd have a major problem with modern concepts of social interaction and friendship. Our nature, which is a social nature, requires real interaction with real people. As a social animal, your kid needs a real "pack" of other human beings in order to be human himself. He is designed to engage people in the real world—not virtual reality.

In the real world, we are biologically limited in the number of friends with whom we can interact. It is impossible to communicate with ten thousand "friends" with one mouth, two eyes and two ears.

In the virtual world, these limits don't obtain. And that can be a dangerous thing.

The Mother Teresa Effect

When asked how she continued to minister to the sick, the poor, and the dying for so many years, Mother Teresa answered, "If I look at the mass, I will never act. If I look at the one, I will."

Think about seeing a starving child in Africa on TV: you flip right by with no problem. But if that kid were on your doorstep, you'd give him food, clothing, and shelter. Getting in front of a person makes him or her real.

The best-selling authors of the book *Made to Stick* coined the phrase "The Mother Teresa Effect" upon learning of a great experiment performed at Carnegie Mellon University. It's all about getting real with people, which is exactly what your kid needs to do.

Researchers at Carnegie Mellon University invited test subjects to fill out a random survey. Upon completion of the survey, they were given five dollars for participating and an envelope containing one of two different fund-raising letters for Save the Children, an organization that helps starving children around the world.

The first letter featured lots of harrowing statistics: three million children were hungry in Malawai; four million Angolans were forced to flee their homes; eleven million Ethiopians needed immediate food assistance.

The second letter focused on a single person, a young girl from Mali named Rokia. The letter described how the money donated would specifically help Rokia with food, education, and medical care.

It turns out that the average person is more like Mother Teresa than he or she realizes. When the test subjects looked at the mass of impoverished children, they donated an average of $1.14. But when they looked at one child, Rokia from Mali, they gave an average of $2.38, or 109 percent more.

The Mother Teresa Effect tells us about more than just our charitable tendencies. It shows that we, as social animals, respond to the real presence of others.

This is why we avoid people we are mad at. It is easier to stay mad at them from a distance. They are less human from a long way away. But in person . . . all of a sudden, we have to judge them less harshly or listen to their side of the story. This goes straight to our human nature as communal animals.

Interacting on Facebook is not the same as interacting "in person." Sure, Facebook is powered by real people, and it has pictures of real people, and it shares news about real people. But socializing on Facebook is not the same as socializing face to face. Beyond the startling statistic that 70 percent of adolescents lie on Facebook, it's just not possible to create and cultivate true friendships through Facebook. Your kid is a real human and deserves real relationships.

Ethan J. Leib, a professor at the University of California-Hastings, wrote in his book *Friend vs. Friend* that longer hours of work and a large amount of online communication such as e-mail and texting take away from personal communication and thus make it much harder to form friendships even in the work place. Furthermore, Facebook and Twitter lessen personal communication. Technology in general, and Facebook and Twitter in particular are making it harder to feel emotional connections to people.

Tweeting vs. Conversation

As of March 2012, Twitter had more than 140 million active users, generating more than 300 million tweets and handling more than 1.6 billion search queries per day. The concept of a "tweet" (for those of you who've been locked in solitary confinement since 2006) is a little noise, like the chirp or tweet of a bird. Tweets consist of only 140 characters in a text-based post. Those last two sentences were more than 170 characters, so you can see how pithy the concept of tweeting is.

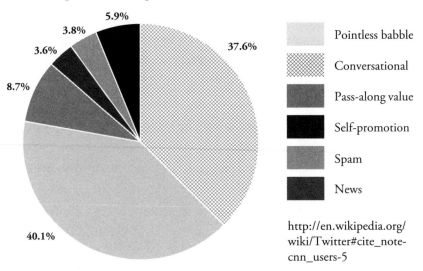

http://en.wikipedia.org/wiki/Twitter#cite_note-cnn_users-5

In 2009 a San Antonio–based market research firm analyzed two thousand tweets, breaking them down into six categories and assigning a percentage to each category.

As you can see pointless babble took first place, with 40 percent. Certain social networking experts took issue with the label "pointless babble," preferring "social grooming" and / or "peripheral awareness." Aristotle would be laughing his toga off at that one, while taking serious issue with calling anything on Twitter "conversation," which took second place at 38 percent.

Is passing back and forth 140 characters true conversation? It reminds me far more of the Borg in *Star Trek*, in which a bio-mechanical race communicates through computer-like declarative statements: "YOU WILL BE ASSIMILATED" or "INDIVIDUALS ARE IRRELEVANT" or "RESISTANCE IS FUTILE."

Your kid is made for more than that. There is nothing wrong per se with Facebook or Twitter, but your kid must understand that this isn't real communication. This might sound obvious to you, but that's because you grew up making a tin can telephone with two empty cans and piece of string.

In part I we discussed how human beings differ from animals, in that humans have rational faculties. A great consequence of rational powers is our ability to engage in real conversation. A hallmark of real conversation is that it engages the highest part of our intellect, which is capable of speculative or theoretical knowledge.

Aristotle says the human mind carries two kinds of knowledge: 1) practical knowledge, and 2) speculative or theoretical knowledge.

Practical knowledge is how to do things. It's the process of learning step by step how to perform a certain function.

Humans and even animals are capable of practical knowledge. A monkey has practical knowledge of how to open a banana. Dogs figure out how to dig a hole under a fence. Humans do both of these, and sometimes not as effectively.

But only humans are capable of pursuing speculative knowledge. Only humans will go to great lengths to learn for the satisfaction merely of knowing. A monkey may make great efforts to climb a towering tree to get the bunch of bananas at the top. But only a human will climb that same tree solely for the purpose of gazing upon a beautiful sunrise that can be seen from the top, content simply to appreciate its majestic beauty.

Aristotle opens his *Metaphysics* with the following:

> All men by nature desire to know. An indication of this is the delight we take in our senses; for even apart from their usefulness they are loved for themselves; *and above all others the sense of sight*. . . . [W]e prefer seeing to everything else. The reason is that this, most of all the senses, makes us know and brings to light many differences between things.

Man was made to see with his speculative mind. But it takes a long time to cultivate this ability. It takes long, deep conversation, and a society taken over by short bursts of communication— like tweeting, texting, and the like—is less and less accustomed to engaging on this level. Still, you've probably experienced the reward of seeing the lightbulb go off in a kid's head after working hard to understand something. This revelation didn't come from tweeting. More likely, it came from good old-fashioned eye contact and conversation.

As a child grows, her mind must address the deeper issues of life. Your kid will confront the difficult issues of love, marriage, religion, politics, and raising kids of her own. Your kid will have to think, and think hard, about these big life issues. Tweeting about these things won't cut it.

What does all this have to do with friendship? Everything. For

Aristotle, friendship is where speculative knowledge is cultivated and best used.

* * *

A while back my wife went on a retreat with a friend, so the two dads, Ryan and me, joined forces to take care of the kids. He's been my best friend since high school.

Here we are, two guys in our early thirties that spent years goofing off in high school and college. Between the two of us, we have nine kids in one house, ten years of age and younger.

Our high school teachers would have thought this was child abuse, given how immature we were then. But we handled the chaos, got all the kids to sleep with a little bribing, and then we found ourselves on my back deck.

It was raining and cool outside, so we turned on the cheap gas fireplace I have on the back deck, and we did what true friends do: we talked. He was holding his newborn, and every few minutes the little guy would squirm or do something cute. Ryan was as happy as I've ever seen him.

But here's the point: we talked about important things, not *how to do things*. We talked about marriage and fatherhood.

— ARISTOTLE'S CHALLENGE —

See if you have the ability to turn off all electronics tonight. Sit around the dinner table with your family. Eat together in a civilized manner. And *stay at the table in your seats for 30 minutes*. Talk about important things. Ask your kids questions—deep questions. See what they think about God, about life, about politics. If you're like most parents, you will see the following: 1) your kids are far more insightful than you imagined; 2) the younger kids are more willing to engage; 3) YOU are part of the problem, not just your kids. You're antsy, anxious, and you feel the need to "get things done." Just chill out and enjoy your kids.

We talked about priorities in life. We talked about how prayer *creates* more time than it takes. We engaged our speculative reasoning for about two hours with no interruption.

Your kid needs to learn to have these conversations. She needs to learn it from you.

It begins at the dinner table. Do you have real conversations with your kid, even the youngest in the bunch? Do you have speculative conversation about life and how to live a good life, or do you simply engage in practical conversation about "getting things done" and how to "do this" and "do that"? This warrants some soul searching on your part.

Family conversation is a lost art. With the onslaught of TV and game systems and Androids and iPods and iPads and e-mail, we've begun to ignore our own family members. There's too much interruption and too much noise. It's very hard to turn off all the devises and simply talk. Chances are good you've forgotten how. And yet, conversation with a loved one is the hallmark of being human. In a sense, we've forgotten how to be human.

Even Aristotle noted that dinner table conversation is a defining trait of human beings as compared with animals:

> [T]his will be realized in their living together and sharing in discussion and thought; for this is what living together would seem to mean in the case of man, and not as in the case of cattle, feeding in the same place.

Once again, Aristotle is dead on. Is your dinner table just a feeding trough? Or is it where you gather as a family of human beings to be together?

Some species eat together. Some species even raise their young together. How are you different? You are different because these animals lack the ability to join together *in truth*. Notice that "*commun*icate" and "*commun*ity" share the same root word. The most important human community is the family. And this family should communicate in a very special way.

In part III we will discuss how conversation between two friends leads to contemplation of the ultimate truths in life. No, contemplation isn't just for monks and hermits. It's for every human being.

For now, however, you have more practical things to deal with, such as baseball practice and Homecoming dates. Aristotle has ancient wisdom for modern parents on these issues as well. Remember, kids don't change. They were the same then as they are now. And the pros and cons of sports and romance will never, ever go away.

Chapter Eight: *Playlist*

- ▶ Virtual presence is not real presence. You know this, but your kid may not.

- ▶ Remember the *Mother Teresa Effect.* "If I look at the mass, I will never act. If I look at the one, I will."
  - ▷ There is no substitute for *real presence.* Virtual presence online is not real presence.
  - ▷ A kid with ten thousand friends will be very lonely.

- ▶ Tweeting is not conversation.
  - ▷ Your kid was made for deep conversation, not "pointless babble."
  - ▷ Conversation between two friends engages the speculative mind. This can't be done in 140 characters on a screen.

▸ The Aristotle Challenge: Sit at the dinner
table for an 30 minutes with your kids . . .
without electronics. Aristotle Triple Dog
Dares you.

CHAPTER NINE

If Aristotle's Kid Had an iPod

"HE WHO IS UNABLE TO LIVE IN SOCIETY,
OR WHO HAS NO NEED BECAUSE HE IS
SUFFICIENT FOR HIMSELF, MUST BE
EITHER A BEAST OR A GOD."

—ARISTOTLE

YOU DON'T have to look far to find a kid with earbuds jammed into his ears, oblivious to the world. This would concern Aristotle, and it should concern you as a parent. The type of music your kid listens to is important, but we'll get to that later. For now, let's ask: what would Aristotle think of the iPod . . . or Netflix or Xbox?

While Aristotle probably wouldn't condemn any of these outright, let's just say he wouldn't be camping out in front of the Apple Store either. Although, ironically, the slavish devotion to these gadgets that causes us to line up and wait together for their release is about the closest we'll come to fostering friendship and community.

Listening to music is a good and very human activity. So what's the big deal with iPods? For one thing, it's those earbuds. Even if your kid is listening to good music, having earbuds perpetually hanging out of his ears isn't a good thing. It's isolating. If your kid is constantly listening to his iPod, he's not engaging others, and they're not engaging him. He's not taking in the world around him; he's blocking it out.

Beyond that, earbuds send a message. According to David Ormesher, founder of Closerlook, a strategic communications firm, earbuds say, "Unless it's urgent, please do not disturb." Similarly, S. Shyam Sundar, codirector of the Media Effects Research Lab at Penn State, says, "It's a signal that people send whether they do it by design or unwillingly . . . that they are otherwise engaged and they are not ready for communication." Suffice it to say, this isn't good for your kid's moral or intellectual development, and it certainly isn't good for his social development.

Quiet contemplation and time alone to think are by no means bad things, and Aristotle would support them, but jamming out to the iPod all day doesn't quite constitute deep thought. In fact, as both Ormesher and Sundar allude to, pumping music into your head at best clears your mind. In a bustling office, where you need to get work done, that can be a good thing, but when your kid is at the park or on the playground? Not so much. He needs to be engaged, learning how to interact with other kids, making friends, solving problems. In short, he needs to be learning how to be a social human being.

Look at All the Lonely People

Plugging in and checking out opens up a whole world of dangers to your kid. If they're plugged in, they're not engaged with you or their friends. In fact, if they're plugged in all the time, chances are they don't even have friends, and if they want them, they probably don't know how to make them.

You've seen this before. You're on public transportation, or walking down the street, or at the mall, and you're surrounded by a sea of people. And yet there's little to no interaction among them. People are listening to their iPods, or talking on their cell phones, or texting. Everyone is off in their own self-manufactured world. It's certainly a stretch to say that if people would unplug, everybody on the subway would become a thriving community; yet there's no denying that being constantly plugged in closes off (or at least severely limits) social interaction and communication.

But being plugged in has become normal. Commuters on a train are now *expected* to be plugged into something. Next time you're on public transportation, try striking up a conversation with one of your fellow travelers. Chances are they'll give you short answers and desperately try to get back to their music or their texting or their video game. It's now odd to be social. It's the norm to collapse into your own world.

Just because it's the norm, however, doesn't mean it's making people happy. Bernardo Carducci is a psychology professor at Indiana University Southeast and the director of the school's very straightforwardly named Shyness Research Institute. Carducci explains the problem:

> You can get exactly what you want, when you want it. You can have your life on your terms. You can get people to deliver movies to your home. People deliver a pizza in a half hour. You can buy stuff and have them ship it to you overnight. You can go on-line and talk to people who have only your same interests. No more dissenting views. You just delete them—"electronic cleansing"—your own world. The solution is getting out of your own world.

He goes even further by saying that because we tune others out, it's causing us to become selfish and lonely at the same time. We are becoming unable to make friends. Even when our kids (and us, for that matter) unplug, they don't know how to socialize or live within a community, let alone make friends. It's what Carducci calls "the iPod effect." Our kids are conditioned to get exactly what they want, when they want it. The song they want to listen to is immediately available on their iPod. And it's immediately down-loadable on their computer if it's not on their iPod. If they want a pizza, it's there in thirty minutes, just how they want it. The characters they play on their video games move and act and think according to the buttons they push. But even the most pliable of human beings won't do whatever your kid wants all the time.

It's become a sort of culture shock when we unplug. Social interaction requires give and take. It takes unselfishness. It takes understanding. Our kids aren't learning any of this from their iPods. And all that instant gratification simply doesn't cut it all the time. As Carducci says, "When you're sick, you don't want e-mails, you want someone to hold your hand, someone to say, 'Let me get this for you.'" And with the iPod effect, we're forgetting how to do that.

Aristotle Would Unplug His Kid

Nielsen polling data from 2011 reveals some disturbing statistics about how your kid spends his time. Kids aged twelve to seventeen spent an average of 123 hours a month watching TV, talking on the phone, surfing the Internet and watching video online. That's more than five days a month lost to "screens," and that doesn't include their 10 percent share of all video games played and their more than 3,300 texts sent per month. Suffice it to say, the average kid spends more time with his gadgets and TV than he does with other people. And that's not good.

Your kid is a social animal, but in an age of iPods and iPhones and the Internet and TV, it is far too easy for your kid (or even us parents) to plug in and check out of social interaction. You would not find Aristotle's kid at a restaurant for Sunday brunch watching a movie on an iPhone. It blows my mind every time I see a young family with kids plugged in at a restaurant.

Aristotle would say that your kid learns how to interact through interaction. Practice makes perfect. Your kid needs to learn how to carry on a conversation—particularly with adults. Your kid needs to learn that the human being sitting across from her is more interesting than SpongeBob SquarePants. You can help them with this understanding. First, you show them by way of example. Engage your own kid in conversation. Ask her about their interests. Ask her opinions on things that perhaps she knows nothing about. At times, you will be amazed at her answers. Kids are insightful. But you will never learn this if you don't engage them.

> **— UNPLUG YOUR TV —**
>
> According to research done by Neilsen and the Kaiser Family Foundations:
>
> - 71 percent of kids have TVs in their room
> - 66 percent of houses leave the TV on during meals
> - 51 percent of houses have the TV on most of the time
>
> *Unplug! Have a conversation!*

Dr. Phil once said, "You aren't raising kids. You are raising adults." Aristotle would agree completely. Your kid is an adult in the making. She needs your example and instruction on how to socialize like an adult. You must spur them on, however, to engage—particularly in this media-saturated society.

One of the many problems with the iPod world we now live in is that it is far too easy to plug in and check out. It is not all right to check out all the time. Every busy parent knows that the TV is a temptation to become your kid's babysitter. Aristotle would then say that as a parent you must overcome your appetites and allow your reason to dictate the permissible use of technology in your kid's life. Don't outsource your kid's upbringing to TV. Don't outsource your kid's upbringing to the local radio stations or to iTunes. Unplug your kid . . . and engage your kid. She is worth it.

Set Your Kids Loose

So you've unplugged your kids and you've engaged them in real conversation. Now what? First of all, you can send them outside. Even if there are no other kids around, your kid will learn a lot more about himself and the world when you set him loose in the backyard rather than setting him in front of the TV.

Sports are a great substitute for the drone of the TV and the constant presence of the Internet. Your kids get outside and become active with other people. They can also become part of a team. The great thing about a team is that everyone is playing. Everyone has come together for the sake of playing. A group of kids is directed toward one goal. This is a great situation for building community and friendship.

The field, or the court, is also a great place to combat the sense of instant gratification that's such a huge part of the iPod effect. In sports, you often have to sacrifice for the good of the team. Like the basketball player who passes up the shot and the chance at glory to pass it to his open teammate. Or like the lineman in football who blocks play after play so the running back and quarterback can run and pass.

Your kids could also get into scouting, where they come together with other kids to camp and do other activities and tasks. Or take dance lessons, or do gymnastics. Anything really.

Or how about this: just let your kids run wild. Let them build forts in the backyard. Yes, they might slam their thumb with a hammer, but that's good. Let them play in the sandlot with friends. A black eye might appear, but that's good too. Modern parents are overprotective. Granted, we have to know exactly what the kids are doing and where they're doing it at all times. It isn't 1950 anymore. We have to be extra careful. But as your kids get older, set them loose. This is how they will learn to be kids so that one day they'll know how to be adults.

When kids run wild (in a good way), they learn to interact with kids on their level. Mom and dad aren't there, which allows them to start solving their own problems, playing their own games, setting their own rules—making their own friendships.

Chapter Nine: *Playlist*

- ▸ iPods, Netflix, Xbox . . . these all isolate your kid from other human beings. How can your kid become a good human being if he doesn't socialize with them?

- ▸ The "iPod effect" has created an antisocial culture. Kids are literally going through culture shock when they unplug.

- ▸ Teenagers average 123 hours a month watching TV, talking on the phone, surfing the Web, and watching video online . . . NOT including video games and their 3,300 texts per month! Enough said.

▸ Dr. Phil says, "You aren't raising kids. You are raising adults." Your kid must unplug and interact with the world around him. Otherwise he will remain a techno-kid forever.

▸ Send your kid outside to start learning how to be human again. A few bumps and bruises are a good thing.

— CHAPTER TEN —

The Other: From the Sandbox to the Altar

"WISHING TO BE FRIENDS IS QUICK
WORK, BUT FRIENDSHIP IS A
SLOW RIPENING FRUIT."

—ARISTOTLE

GOD FORBID your kid becomes homeless, or that his marriage falls apart, or that he becomes obese from overeating. Luckily, you've got some say in the matter. These tragedies often occur, in large part, because people lack true friendships. They don't have true friends to keep them on the right path or tell them to stop eating a carton of Twinkies a day. Or they didn't marry a true friend. Sure, there are other factors, but more often than not, people who find themselves in these unhappy states feel unloved—without a friend.

But if the lack of friendship is a cause of so many tragedies, surely the tragedies will dwindle away soon! With Twitter and Facebook and texting and e-mail, we have a thousand ways to make a thousand friends, right? Wrong. As a parent, it's vital that you know this: friendship—real, true friendship—is on the decline in America.

In June 2006, a study was published in the *American Sociological Review* that showed Americans (as opposed to other nationalities) are suffering from a decline in quality friendships since at least 1985. As of 2006, 25 percent of Americans said they have no close "confidants." And since 1985, the average total number of confidants per citizen has dropped from four to two.

— MORE STATS FROM *AMERICAN SOCIOLOGICAL REVIEW* —

▶ Americans with at least one confidant not connected through kinship dropped from 80 percent to 57 percent.

▶ Americans' dependence on a spouse went up from 5 percent to 9 percent, which means fewer friends outside the home.

▶ A link was found between having fewer friends and psychological regression.

▶ The unusually high divorce rate in America causes people to lose friends via divorced spouses; i.e., the friend sides with one spouse or the other.

Americans are losing friends left and right, even though our standard of what constitutes a "friend" is much less than a true, Aristotelian friend.

Aristotle believed that friendship, particularly true friendship, was the remedy to many problems in life. "In poverty and other misfortunes of life, true friends are a sure refuge," he said. A true friend provides a good at the right time and in the right way. Friends "keep the young out of mischief," he says. As the old saying goes, "Idle hands are the devil's tools." Kids are no different today than they were in ancient Greece. They must stay busy, *real busy*, to stay out of trouble. Of course, pleasure friendships among kids can lead to broken windows, dangerous forts, blown-up Barbie convertibles, and more. Therefore, the job of a parent is to find constructive, fun things for little kids to do with friends.

As your kids grow older, Aristotle says that true friends move each other "to noble deeds." Here lies the highest form of friendship. The most perfect friendship helps each friend strive for virtue. But your kid doesn't have to wait until adulthood to develop a true friendship, as we will address momentarily.

For now, however, remember that today's most cutting-edge research is proving Aristotle right on the importance of friendship for a virtuous and happy life. If your kid's best friend eats healthily, your kid will be five times more likely to eat a healthy diet. If he gets married, he will say that friendship is five times more important than physical intimacy with his spouse. And if he doesn't feel that he has true friends at work, he will have just a one in twelve chance of feeling engaged in his job. Amazingly, if he has a good friend at work, he will be seven times more likely to feel engaged. Clearly, friendship is monumentally important in life . . . and it starts in the sandbox.

*   *   *

Earlier, we looked at the three prerequisites for true friendship:

1. Both people must be virtuous;
2. Both must people care more about loving than being loved.
3. You can have only a few true friends.

True friendship is the most perfect between two adults. In fact, it is most perfect between man and woman in the bond of marriage. But, to a limited extent, even rug rats can partake in all three aspects of true friendship. So let's begin in the sandbox and work our way through different stages of life up to holy matrimony.

In the Sandbox

One of your kid's first words was probably "mine." "Gimme" probably came shortly after. If you're a parent, the following scenario may be familiar: you or an older sibling takes a toy or cell phone away from the little one. Then an anger erupts that resembles a diabolical possession. The entire body tightens and begins to shake; the teeth clinch to the point of grinding; the fists ball up and are raised to the air; the face becomes red and then purple; an escalating scream begins, causing onlookers to believe an amputation has just occurred. Lunacy has taken over. For a moment you wonder if she will vomit across the room as her head slowly spins 360 degrees.

It is not uncommon. If your child has humiliated you in public in this way, have no fear—she is normal. Toddlers have no other way to communicate. They know what they want but can't say it. They can point, they can scream, they can bite an enemy, but their rationality has not fully developed, and their passions are in command. Such behavior is most noticeable when your kid is interacting with other playmates. The sandbox is where we learn that our kids are animals, albeit rational animals.

This "mine" mentality, however, can be slowly replaced with a "yours" mentality. It is in the sandbox where babies become students of philosophy, and moms the great orators of truth. Moms and dads throughout all of history have been squatting down in the sandbox next to their toddler and saying, "Let's share with your friend." It is here where friendship training begins.

Two types of parents drive me crazy at the sandbox. On the one hand, you have parents who don't control their kids at all. You know the type. Little Johnny was diagnosed with ADHD when he was three weeks old because he woke up crying at 3 a.m. Therefore, he gets to bully everyone else's kids. On the other hand, you have parents who enter into an elaborate dialogue with their two-year-old about morals and ethics. As always, the virtue is found between the extremes. Aristotle would say use the sandbox—the playground, playdates, siblings, and every other interaction—as a way for your kid to learn that the world does not revolve around him or her. In fact, the sandbox doesn't either!

Little kids, even those still in diapers, can begin to develop the requirements of true friendship. In true friendship, you'll remember, "both people care more about loving than being loved." This may sound like the most difficult requirement for a toddler to grasp, but it is in fact the easiest. Even little kids know that being good makes other people happy. They can quickly learn that giving is more rewarding than receiving. Selfishness is of course present in every kid and takes years to uproot, but the idea that giving is better than receiving is also present. It just needs some encouraging. Sharing her toys, throwing away the paper towel as mommy's "special helper," or giving hugs and kisses to daddy as he goes to work are ways for little kids to develop friendships at a young age. It's not yet true friendship, and it may be only with mommy and daddy, but the little flickers of friendship are beginning to glow.

In the Sandlot

In the movie *The Sandlot*, there's a great scene in which the rich kids on the organized baseball team confront the kids who play on the sandlot.

A kid named Phillips, the ring leader of the rich kids, gets into it with Benny, the best of the sandlot players. It soon becomes a match of "wits," the insults escalating in typical adolescent grossness, until Ham Porter, the catcher, ends it: "You play ball like a giiiirrrlll."

It's the last straw. An insult so horrifying that both sides are silenced. It leads to a baseball game the next day that will settle the dispute once and for all.

Believe it or not, this is exactly how your kid learns to develop friends—crass insults and all.

In the sandbox, mommy is there to settle all disputes over the plastic shovel. She intervenes to protect her baby from the bully. But in the sandlot—where the older kids play—mom and dad aren't present. The kids choose the teams. The kids call balls and strikes. The kids exercise justice and mercy. The kids come to the defense of their own friends against the stuck-up punks like Phillips. The team captains learn in the sandlot how to run the business they'll have twenty years later. And it's where boys and girls learn how to be good men and women, which eventually leads to being good husbands and wives.

The sandlot represents the bridge between being a baby in the sandbox and being an adult out in the world. Your adolescent kid develops a very deep and abiding notion of friendship during these years. Adolescents may not develop true friendships—the type Aristotle has in mind for adults—but they do begin to develop in a limited way the three requirements for true friendship.

Both people must be virtuous

I have noticed that once my kids reach the age of reason, generally considered to be around seven, they can appreciate and desire goodness in their playmates. They clearly dislike selfish playmates, or bullies, or know-it-alls.

A ten-year-old boy, for example, can begin to see the moral character of playmates, although he may not be able to articulate it very well. Likewise, a ten-year-old can certainly learn that his own moral character can be attractive or unattractive to other people. It is incumbent upon mom and dad constantly to remind their kids that good people like other good people.

It's also important for parents to actively open the door of friendship to their kids. If your kid seems to like another kid who *you* think is a good moral influence, it is important to actively foster their friendship.

Both people must care more about loving than being loved

Once a friendship begins to take shape (in kids, it will generally start as a pleasure friendship), remind your kid that giving is more important *and more enjoyable* than receiving. Help them put that principle into action by sharing, listening rather than talking, praising rather than criticizing, or even praying for the other person when he does something mean.

If your kid is old enough to be deeply hurt by another, then he is old enough to focus on giving rather than receiving. It sounds counterintuitive, but the fastest and easiest way to heal the wounds of adolescent cruelty is to be kind to the other. Socrates's famous words come to mind: "It is better to suffer injustice than commit it." And this is true even for middle school kids. Teaching your kids to love everyone—enemies and friends—no matter the circumstances, is key to their moral development.

You can have only a few true friends

Your kid might have a "best friend" every other week. That's normal, but it's important to slowly introduce the concept that true friends are rare, even at an elementary school age. Kids know that rare things are valuable, that treasure is hard to find. It is easy to explain to your kid that a true friend, a very best friend, is very rare indeed. True friendship is something *so special* that it can be shared with only a few people.

* * *

The sandlot—that bridge between the sandbox and the adult world—is where your kids learn that good people are better to be with, that giving is better than receiving, and that true friends are hard to come by.

These early friendships formed on the sandlots and playgrounds teach your kid about humanity. A twelve-year-old boy learns a lot about life and humanity from his best buddy. It is in these volatile years that emotions run high, that boys and girls learn more about themselves, their own passions, their strengths and weaknesses. And with every passing year, the friendships they forge seem to raise the stakes.

Eventually, dating will come up. There is no avoiding it. But Aristotle would say that some of the work in preparing your kid for dating and romance has already been done. Dating is a friendship, and because your kid—with your help—has been pursuing good friendships all his life, he'll be better prepared to date. But what's the purpose of dating?

At the Prom

Aristotle begins his *Ethics* with one of the most famous lines in all of history: "[E]very action and pursuit is thought to aim at some good." This may sound simple, but it's very profound. This entire book is about helping your kids find the good, the end, the goal in life. As a parent, it's your responsibility to teach your kid the purpose of their actions and constantly to remind them that the final destination is true happiness. Too many parents allow their kids to wander aimless amid the tossing waves of life. It's like leaving your child on a small raft with no food or water, never having taught them to guide their way by the stars, never pointing them toward shore. If they're lucky, someone else's ship will rescue them, but your kids are too important to leave it up to luck.

It's no surprise that your kid's strongest passions will probably be sexual in nature. A teenager's sexual passions are more like a hurricane with fierce winds and piercing rain than mild waves in the ocean. But it is even worse than that. A teenager in today's culture and dating scene is faced with a perfect storm.

The first major difficulty for the typical teenager is his powerful passions, especially the sex drive. Couple this with the typical teenager's know-it-all attitude and you have strong passions being driven by a stupid mind. This difficulty is nothing new.

Some kids, some cultures, deal with this better than others. As we discussed in part I, passions are good, but they must be directed by reason. We should not be Stoics. We should not see sex as a necessary evil for procreation. Your child should not be ashamed of his physical development in puberty, nor the typical passions that come along with this development. But we do need to show our kids the "good" for which these passions were made. It's difficult for a teenager to understand marriage and all the bells and whistles that go along with it, but they can understand true friendship. They can understand that passions take true friendship to another level of perfection and that this is only possible within the confines of marriage—the greatest friendship of all.

The passions—and the sexual drive—are a part of human nature. What makes the whole thing tougher for kids today is the second part of the perfect storm: our sex-obsessed culture. Every street corner, every shopping mall, every magazine rack, every popular TV show, is cluttered with sexual images.

I remember traveling in Germany in the 1990s and being amazed that full nudity was on billboards across the street from office buildings, churches, and schoolyards. The Judeo-Christian values on which America was built have held the barbarians at the gate as long as they could. But it seems the battle has been lost. Modesty is all but a forgotten term, let alone a virtue, and there's virtually no effort to promote chastity. Pornography is everywhere and has become, more or less, an accepted part of society. No matter how much you protect your children, they will encounter a filthy world.

That's why it's so important to arm your kid against the storm that's raging against him. You can help him weather the storm by discussing the purpose of sex *at an appropriate age.* In Aristotle's words, keep the end in mind. Is the end self-gratification? Is the purpose of other people to provide you pleasure? Are women objects for entertainment? Is sex nothing more than two people using each other for self-gratification? Of course not.

Imagine saying to your daughter, "I hope you find someone whom you can use and who can use you for physical amusement"? I've never heard the father of the bride at a wedding toast his daughter by saying, "May you use each other until the end of your days." If this sounds ridiculous, it's because it is. But if you think your son or daughter deserve more than this, then you better start thinking about what your kids' bodies are for. The culture says they're for pleasure—PERIOD.

This is the storm you and your kid are up against. And we're so deep within it that it's often hard to break out. We have a multi-generational lineage of sexual insanity. The sexual revolution of the 1960s is still having its effect. Baby Boomers danced naked at Woodstock. Generation X grew up with sex idols like Madonna and perverts like Prince. And as these gen-Xers became professional adults, Internet porn busted at the seams and set the stage for their new addiction. Generation Y came along with no concept of anything other than what was laid before them. In other words, your kid has a parent infected with the sexual values of generation

X or generation Y. Even if you escaped into adulthood without these values, you've spent your whole life surrounded by them, and so have your kids.

It's important to understand that you come from a perverse generation. If you think premarital sex is OK, please note that your thought is a result of weed-smoking hippies dancing naked in the mud. Civilized societies going back thousands of generations (not just years) have believed in waiting for marriage. Of course, fornication has always been around, but very few cultures have condoned it until recently.

As a parent, you can't give in to the current culture. You can't think in terms of the most recent forty or fifty years. Rather, think in terms of fort thousand or fifty thousand years of human history. Your kid is worth far more than 1969 morality.

*   *   *

So your kid's facing a perfect storm when it comes to dating. Great. What's the answer then? What's dating for? Is it for sexual experimentation? Carnal pleasure? We've established that your kids are worth more than that.

The end, or goal, of dating is preparation for marriage. Note that the end of dating is not marriage itself. Not every dating relationship needs to—or should—end in marriage. Every dating relationship should, however, better prepare your kid for marriage. If it doesn't, it's a waste of time and potentially dangerous.

Dating denotes some form of a budding romance. That is clear. But it is not a pleasure friendship or a utility friendship. It is something different, something much more serious. In a similar way, a marriage is something more than a true friendship. It contains the element of a true friendship, but it is more.

Dating must remain focused on its purpose: to better prepare one for marriage. It is an opportunity for a young man and young woman to get to know each other on a deep, personal level. It can provide the setting for each to enjoy open conversation about life, about God, about work, about family and culture. It is an opportunity to learn more about the other sex (aside from those annoying siblings at home). Dating is that opportunity to learn why God made man and woman and why both are in His image.

Aristotle would agree that dating is a means to an end. Dating is preparation for marriage. But when should that preparation start? There's no exact answer to when your kid should start dating, but with Aristotle's help, I can provide some basic points for you to consider.

To tie the knot, Aristotle would say a couple must be able to develop a "true friendship." So, too, for dating. Dating is preparation for marriage, which is the highest form of true friendship. It stands to reason, then, that your kid must have the ability to pursue true friendship in order to date.

The fact is that no one is ready to get married until he or she gets married. And no one's ready to date until he or she is ready to date. The best preparation, therefore, is found in Aristotle's requirements for true friendship, and that develops over time. It starts in the sandbox, and then on the sandlot, and it continues through high school and college, and in dating. All these friendships prepare your kids for the ultimate friendship with their spouse.

While Aristotle wouldn't recommend a specific age that's right for dating, he would want his son to understand on a relatively deep level that marriage, and therefore dating, is not about the self; it is about the other. Parents think about a million different things regarding dating, but it comes down to this: is my kid able to give himself unconditionally to another person? If the answer is no, then they're not ready.

Aristotle's principles provide us with a framework for dating. The purpose or "end" of dating is preparation for marriage. And friendship is the best preparation, not hooking up. Of course, kids are limited in how deep their friendship can be, but they can begin desiring the good for their best friend and experience the joy that comes from loving another in a selfless way.

Eventually, the young adult befriends someone of the other sex who looks a little different than them. He begins to get a little nervous around her. The stomach stirs. The heart flutters. And the mind becomes fixated. And perhaps one day, a bunch of little Aristotles will be running around the living room.

To the Altar

Soon after I had my first child, my dad gave me some excellent advice: "The best thing you can do for your son is love his mother." I think Aristotle would agree.

One of your primary goals as a parent should be to help pre-pare your child for the most important relationship in his or her life, namely, marriage. Here a picture is truly worth a thousand words. You could try to sit your one-year-old in the high chair and explain the concept of unconditional love, but you'd just get Cheerios tossed in your face. Your infant doesn't understand any of that. But they watch. When two parents argue, the one-year-old sees it. And amazingly, they understand. Remember, your kid is a social animal with tremendous sensitivity to the people around him. He doesn't understand the conversation, but he senses peace and he senses friction. An animal that loses its herd is incomplete. It is lost. It is afraid. And so are children stricken by divorce.

Here's an amazing statistic from Dr. Nicholas Wolfinger from the University of Utah: if you (the parent) get divorced, your kid is 40 percent more likely to get divorced. But it gets worse: if you (the parent) remarry, your kid is 91 percent more likely to get divorced.

The best lesson you can give your kid about marriage is living the virtues of true friendship with your own spouse.

Aristotle wouldn't be surprised by these stats. Our social natures soak in everything around us. Just as the college students in the Stanford Experiment became in their own minds real guards and prisoners, just as kids in the Bobo Doll Experiment take on the characteristics of the adults in the room within minutes, your kid will take on many of your own attitudes toward marriage.

Why does remarriage increase the likelihood of divorce? There is no clear answer. Perhaps a child learns that getting a new spouse is an option when the first one gets old, just like getting a new car when the first one breaks down.

But these statistics don't prove that divorce is actually harmful to the kid. They only show that divorce is passed down from generation to generation. Well then, here is a stat that will knock your socks off. Dr. Robert E. Emery, professor of psychology and director of the Center for Children, Families and the Law at the University of Virginia, has made it his life's work to study the impact of divorce on families, particularly children. He is also the father of five children. In his book *Marriage, Divorce, and Children's Adjustment*, which won the prestigious Outstanding Academic Book award from *Choice* magazine, Dr. Emory determined that children of divorce suffer more psychological problems than children that suffer a death in the family.

Aristotle would nod his head in agreement. After all, it was he who said friendship is more important than life itself: "Without friends, no one would choose to live, even though he had all other goods." Children who suffer through a divorce experience something worse than death; they experience the death of friendship. They witness mom and dad, who are supposed to be the most important people in the world to each other, voluntarily break away. Children sense a spiritual death, which is exactly what divorce is. Marriage creates a new entity. It is something different from the husband and wife individually. Divorce, then, is the death of this spiritual union and creation, which is even more difficult for a child to witness than the physical death of a loved one. In physical death, even a child knows that the spirit can live on. But when the spirit dies, the body—the physical presence of mom and dad—does not suffice.

Additionally, kids have a friendship of sorts with this third entity: the marriage. Kids don't know mom simply as mom; they know her as the other half of dad. Kids don't know dad simply as dad; they know him as the other half of mom. And kids are bound to this mom/dad union. When this union falls apart, kids lose a friendship with the union. Although the relationship with mom and dad individually can continue, it is not the same.

Divorce affects not only little kids. It also affects big kids. In 2000, Dr. Emery performed a survey of college students whose parents had divorced at least three years prior. Some of these students may have been little kids when the divorce occurred. Some may have been early high school age. The point of the study, however, is that college kids are still feeling the pain of divorce.

Your marriage is a profound influence on your kid's well-being now and in the future. It will affect all his friendships, from the ones in the sandbox all the way up to his spouse. First things first, mom and dad: *the best thing you can do for your kid is to love your spouse.*

* * *

Finally, our discussion of true friendship and marriage ends with a twist. All this talk about giving rather than receiving, and loving the other for his or her own sake, and yet, the final point is this: *marriage is far more than just the other person.* The best marriages, the most perfect friendships, have another agenda at work other than the good for the other person. And in a sense, it is a selfish motive. Some philosophers have called this the "Transcendent Third," but we'll simply call it "the Other."

Aristotle says that when two people come together in true friendship, they desire *the good* for the other person. This good could be as simple as a good night's sleep or as beautiful as a happy baby. But the more virtuous a man or a woman is, the more he or she understands what the *real goods* are in life. Both learn that being virtuous *is* a reward in itself. And they desperately desire their true friend to experience the joy and happiness that results from virtue.

But Aristotle also says that true friends come together, not only for each other, but also for some *absolute good*. This absolute good is beyond either person in the friendship. This *absolute good* simply cannot be given or received from one another. Again, one cannot give what one does not have. The most loving wife in the world cannot give absolute goodness, for she is far from perfect herself. She can give only shadows of goodness itself. A loving husband cannot show his wife absolute truth or absolute beauty, for he has only a glimmer of truth within his soul and has seen only reflections of beauty itself.

Still, a truly virtuous person seeks the absolutes—the best—not mere shadows and reflections. We were made for more than our spouse—and a loving spouse knows this better than anyone.

Aristotle believed that true friendship was not stable if it was bound together only by each other. Rather, true friends are uniting forces as they soar upward toward the Other that transcends everything else. Aristotle did not benefit from the Judeo-Christian revelation and so had a hard time figuring out exactly what this Other was. But he knew that something else was up there.

A sacramental marriage is truly the most perfect example of true friends coming together for their own happiness, for each other's happiness, but also for The Other, namely God—the *Absolute*.

He is Truth, Goodness, and Beauty itself. There is nothing beyond Him. There is no more final end to seek. In the end, a spouse is also a means to another end: God. It is with God that a truly perfect friendship can exist, and nowhere else.

Chapter Ten: *Playlist*

- *In the Sandbox*, kids learn that "MINE" is not always acceptable. "YOURS" is better.
  - ▷ Mommy becomes the philosopher teaching her kid right from wrong.

- *In the Sandlot*, kids learn to fight, insult and get in trouble. But they also learn to set rules, to lead others, to work as a team.
  - ▷ *The Sandlot* teaches more about friendship than baseball.

- *At the Prom* you will find scary business. Remember the "perfect storm" of our sex-crazed culture.
  - ▷ Dating is a "means" to marriage. Marriage is the "end." Aristotle would say if dating doesn't help you prepare for marriage in some way, it is harmful.

- *To the Altar* is hopefully where your kid will go. It is here he or she will find true friendship with a spouse, and then to the ultimate "Other."

— Part III —

Happiness

"Happiness is the highest good."

—Aristotle

CHAPTER ELEVEN

The Real Role of Pleasure

"THE PLEASURE PROPER TO A WORTHY
ACTIVITY IS GOOD AND THE PLEASURE
PROPER TO AN UNWORTHY ACTIVITY IS BAD."
—ARISTOTLE

Aristotle vs. Tony Robbins

IMAGINE THE music is pumping, the crowd is cheering. There are fireworks and flashing lights. As the song blares on, the crowd rises and begins clapping, bobbing up and down in fitful anticipation. Finally, out runs Tony Robbins, the man of the hour. The crowd erupts, and he plays into it, galloping about the stage, clapping his hands, revving the crowd even more. Finally, with one big sweep of his hands he calls for silence in the stadium.

This is the man they've been waiting for. This is the guy with all the answers. He will tell them to stand. They will. He will ask them to raise their hands. They will. He'll ask someone to recount a deeply personal, even embarrassing story. They will tell Tony Robbins what many people wouldn't even bring to the confessional.

127

And why not? He's the guy with all the answers. After pumping up and calming down the crowd a few more times, Robbins declares: "If at any point during the first day of this seminar, you want to leave, go ahead. You'll get your money back. No questions asked." Nobody leaves.

So he begins: "The way to achieve your goals . . . to become happy . . . to be successful . . . to be the person you want to be . . ." He pauses for dramatic effect, and the crowd, including Aristotle, leans forward in anticipation. Robbins flashes a leathery grin and continues, ". . . is to seek pleasure and avoid pain. That's the great motivator. To seek pleasure and avoid pain."

At this point, Aristotle hikes up his toga and sprints for the exit.

*   *   *

Pleasure in itself isn't bad. Many good things are pleasant. Bodily pleasures are nice, and there are far more pleasant things too. Good things. But pleasure is not happiness, and the two must not be confused. Pleasure gets a lot of attention because it's a short cut we think will lead to happiness—but it won't. Tony Robbins's philosophy is regurgitated pablum that's been sold many times before.

Imagine if the movie *Star Wars* were released every year with the same script and the same effects but with new character names. Instead of Luke Skywalker, the hero's name is Jude Airrunner. The following year his name is Miles Cloudjumper. And the next year, Brady Spaceflyer. If someone had never seen *Star Wars* before and knew nothing about the great saga and heroism of Luke Skywalker, they might be impressed with Brady Spaceflyer. But to someone who grew up playing with Luke Skywalker toys and running through his mother's kitchen with the *Millennium Falcon* and Han Solo, Brady Spaceflyer is simply a cheesy remake.

A philosopher would likewise roll his eyes at the sight and sound of yet another hedonistic philosopher like Tony Robbins. But we must give Tony some credit for uniqueness—he does have bigger biceps than his thousands of predecessors. Congrats, Tony! Well done!

What precisely is wrong with the philosophy of hedonism, which says to seek pleasure and avoid pain. Isn't pleasure good? Isn't pain bad? Sure, on some level at least. But happiness is not that simple.

Aristotle took these questions head on more than 2,300 years ago. He looked at virtuous people to see what they enjoyed. This makes sense. If you want to know what food is healthy, for example, look at what athletes and fit people eat. If you want to know what makes a good investment, study the business activities of the rich. And if you want to know what is truly pleasurable, look to those who truly enjoy life . . . not just during momentary "highs" but in an enduring and sustained way.

Part of your job as a parent is to show your kids people who enjoy life—and to enjoy it yourself! These people have the right pleasures, and they don't take advice from Tony Robbins. They know that life is more than avoiding pain.

Do they like pain? No. As the great philosopher Joseph Pieper says, " 'Suffering for its own sake' is nonsense." The people you know who have deep-seated contentment have suffered in ways and continue do so, but for good reason. They know that Tony is missing something. That something is the journey toward happiness that involves many ups and downs, many pains and sorrows, but also great joy and happiness. Rejecting pain outright is not the answer. The answer is to seek the good, embrace the suffering for good reason, and ultimately to find virtue and happiness on the other side.

The Lord of the Rings *and the Ring of Gyges*

In *The Lord of the Rings*, a hobbit named Smeagol famously murdered his friend to obtain a ring of great power. Over the years, Smeagol became known as Gollum, so called because of the guttural noise he made while obsessing over the ring.

Gollum's love for the ring completely consumed him. All he wanted was to be alone with his "Precious." This obsession with the ring, mixed with its inherent evil, first distorted his mind, and eventually began to distort his body. He lived far beyond his natural life span but with no quality of life.

The ring had the power to make its bearer disappear—and eventually fade out of existence. Had he continued to wear it, Gollum would have vanished completely. The ring literally consumed Gollum's life. And he began to hate it, though he remained enslaved to the lust for the power that his "Precious" gave him. Gollum's love affair with the ring is what we all go through with vice.

Consider the married man who enjoys going to Hooters for the "view." Soon this turns into a few late nights at the Paper Doll lounge with his buddies, then an affair with a girl at work, which results in a divorce.

This young married man took off his ring of fidelity to his wife and put on the ring of pleasure, disappearing during his lunch breaks as he walked into Hooters, disappearing a bit longer on Friday nights at the Paper Doll lounge, and eventually disappearing altogether from his wife and children.

So what does this have to do with your kids? As a parent, you must show them that putting on vice and sin slowly erases their true selves. Sin, even at a tender age, begins the slow and painful process of destroying what God created.

Your kid is encouraged by every commercial, by every billboard, by every contact with the secular world, to "seek pleasure."

You are raising your kid in the Age of Indulgence. And because of this extra dose of temptation your kid is receiving every day, you must counteract this with an extra dose of temperance.

Your kid will face a very big question in life: Are you going to do what is good, or are you going to do what feels good? The ancient Greeks dealt with this very question and so will future generations. In fact, Aristotle's teacher, Plato, taught extensively on it, with a story that serves as a precursor to *The Lord of the Rings*.

In his most famous work, the *Republic*, Plato discusses virtue and temptation with a guy named Glaucon. Glaucon sounds like most modern thinkers. He says that if a man were given the ability to perform any act without being known or discovered, he would indulge his every desire, checking virtue at the door. In other words, Glaucon believes that the only reason we behave well is because of social pressure. He argues that we desire the reputation of being virtuous more than actually being virtuous.

Glaucon tells the story of the Ring of Gyges to illustrate his point. Gyges of Lydia, a lowly shepherd for the great King Candaules, was tending his flock when an earthquake opened up an entrance to a mysterious cave. Gyges explored the cave and discovered it was a hidden tomb of a corpse wearing a golden ring. Gyges could not resist taking the ring, and eventually he learned that the ring could make him disappear, giving him great power.

Gyges used his newfound power to seduce the Queen of Lydia and, with her help, murder the king. Thus, Gyges the shepherd became King Gyges.

Glaucon argues that all of us, including you and your kid, are no better than Gyges. If the social constraints of morality are cast aside, he says, there is nothing stopping your kid from lying, cheating, and even killing:

> No man can be imagined to be of such an iron nature
> that he would stand fast in justice. No man would keep
> his hands off what was not his own when he could safely
> take what he liked out of the market, or go into houses
> and lie with any one at his pleasure, or kill or release
> from prison whom he would, and in all respects be like
> a god among men. (Plato's *Republic*, 360, Jowett trans.)

Glaucon goes even further. Suppose a man had the power to do whatever he wanted. And suppose this man did not use his power for pleasure, but tried to live virtuously. What would others think of him? Glaucon says this:

> If you could imagine any one obtaining this power
> of becoming invisible, and never doing any wrong or
> touching what was another's, he would be thought by
> lookers-on to be a most wretched idiot, although they
> would praise him to one another's faces. . . . (Ibid.)

What do teenagers think of a guy who refuses to smoke a joint, or a girl who says she will remain a virgin. When you were a teenager and a classmate stood up for something noble or went against the crowd and remained honest or chaste, did you conclude they were "a most wretched idiot"?

Or did something inside of you admire this person? Did a little voice say, "She's right. You should do the same."

Plato argues that Gyges isn't representative of every man, but rather of a man who has enslaved himself to his desires. Gyges, like Gollum, let his passions control his reason. Although we don't know about Gyges's future happiness, Gollum became a miserable creature, eaten away by his own insatiable desire for pleasure.

Plato insists there are men who could possess the power of Gyges and remain virtuous because their reason controls their passions. Here is where Aristotle goes beyond Plato. Plato thought the passions had to be ruled, and we often take this approach with our kids: "Control your emotions!" we might chide our kids. But Aristotle has a different view. He believes we can convert our wild emotions into virtuous emotions. He believes that through hard work and right reasoning, your kid can develop good emotions, and use them to drive toward a virtuous and happy life.

So what then is the proper role of pleasure? Is seeking pleasure bad? How should you as a parent help your kid understand pleasure? Since we live in the Age of Indulgence, these may be among the most important questions you ask.

The Real Role of Pleasure

Pleasure is what immoral people have. Pain is what moral people have. Right? Wrong! The world will try to convince your kid of this, but nothing could be further from the truth.

Remember, if doing something isn't easy, it isn't a virtue. Aristotle says that forming habits makes doing good easier, and even pleasurable. Otherwise, you are merely strong-willed and have to work through the struggle. Does "being good" take work? Yes. Is it sometimes hard? Yes. But most good things in life are. Eventually, however, it becomes easier and more pleasurable, far more pleasurable than transitory desires.

Your kid needs to see that difficulty does not negate pleasure. If it did, why would kids love playing football? Why do they want to get hit? Because there is great pleasure in the game. Watch a climber scaling a cliff. Does he wince in pain when he's in a tough spot, looking for that next hold? Yes. Does he still find it pleasurable? Absolutely. The reality is that pain does not eliminate pleasure or happiness.

You do your kid a huge disservice if you let him think that

pleasure is either the most important thing in the world or a synonym for evil. As always, the truth lies in the middle. Pleasure can be good, or pleasure can be bad. If the pleasure is directed toward an evil, it is always bad. If it is a moderate pleasure directed toward a good then it certainly can be morally good.

Your kid was made to enjoy life. But you must distinguish between raw, carnal, short-lived pleasure, and a deeper, long-lasting pleasure. The world is full of short-lived, damaging pleasures. You've got to show your kid the true joy of deep pleasure and the harm that fleeting pleasures can cause. It is one of the most important things you'll ever do.

The Necessity of Health, Wealth, and Reputation

Aristotle is the father of moderation, and so he has a very balanced and insightful understanding of the necessity of worldly things. Aristotle believed that life was made for more than mere amusement and that living a virtuous life and having true friendships lead to true happiness. Pleasure, wealth, and honor do have their roles but are not sufficient for happiness. Just as pleasure friendships are good and valuable and part of true friendship, so too is pleasure part of true happiness. You just can't stop at pleasure.

> Christianity shifts away from Aristotle's thinking on "worldly things." They are still not bad in themselves. In fact, they are good. But with God (with Christ), they are not necessary for happiness. Remember Jesus' words to the man who asked him how to become perfect: "If you would be perfect, go, sell what you possess and give to the poor, and you will have treasure in heaven; and come follow me." (Matthew 19:21)

Aristotle was not naïve. He knew that people, particularly

young people, were inclined toward pleasure. It is easy for youth to equate pleasure and happiness. The raw sensation of physical pleasure can blind young people from seeing the true happiness that lies on the other side of virtue.

Aristotle is not an idealist. He's very practical. He understands that certain things are necessary for happiness. Remember that Aristotle was not a Jew or a Christian and that he had no supernatural revelation or sacramental grace to elevate him beyond the natural level of things. Thus, everything he says is within the natural level. Aristotle said that certain conditions were required to obtain true happiness. Some examples include:

Health

In Aristotle's mind, a severe bodily or mental illness would create such a disharmony in one's being that a constant struggle would exist. Health is important so that one isn't constantly distracted by pain. This doesn't just mean being free from disease. It also relates to our day-to-day health. Are we (and our kids) active? Do we eat well? Studies have shown that obesity can lead to depression, and yet we still tend to binge eat while watching TV, and our kids have a hard time entertaining themselves without an Xbox and a bunch of snacks.

It's important to live a healthy and active life in order to achieve happiness. When your body is healthy, your soul is more likely to be healthy as well.

Wealth

The only people in the world who say "money doesn't matter" are people that have a ton of it or people that have none of it. Aristotle knows you need the right amount of it. Aristotle knows that the "right amount" is enough to provide you with shelter, health, education, and leisure. Leisure is good, but it doesn't mean lying around on the couch watching TV for five hours. Rather, it involves using your talents recreationally but also in a way that is productive and beneficial.

Money is good because it can help you obtain other good things in life. Too much money distracts you because you become focused on keeping it or what to do with it. Too little money prevents you from enjoying it because you are too busy making sure you have enough. The middle ground means just enough. Obviously this requires further self-discipline and "virtue" in financial dealings by not desiring too many things and by keeping your priorities straight and being content with a simple life.

Reputation

People want to love others, but frankly we also want to be loved. This is not bad. As we said before, a true friend cares more about loving than being loved, but he still wants to be loved. Aristotle knows that your social status is important. If people think poorly of you, it easily sends you into a dark place. To be truly happy, we need a reasonably good reputation. Your kid wants to be liked, and parents should encourage this desire.

While Aristotle stressed the importance of having health, wealth, and reputation, they are not sufficient for happiness. For Aristotle, they are necessary for happiness, but they do not suffice.

So, while health, wealth, and reputation—and other pleasures—are important for happiness, according to Aristotle, and even today, they don't make us happy by themselves. What else do we need?

Chapter Eleven: *Playlist*

- ▸ The Tony Robbins recipe for happiness— "Seek pleasure and avoid pain"—is old news.

- ▸ Pleasure isn't bad. It can be very good. But it is *not* synonymous with happiness.

- ▸ Remember the Ring of Gyges: if your kid had great power, would he use it for his own pleasure or for doing good? In *The Lord of the Rings*, Gollum used his ring for pleasure, which made him fade from existence.

- ▸ The real role of pleasure is to enjoy good things once you have trained your emotions to enjoy them.

- ▸ Health, wealth, and reputation are pleasurable and necessary, to a limited extent, to be truly happy.

CHAPTER TWELVE

The Cardinal Virtues:
Opening and Closing the Door to Happiness

"WE PURSUE . . . ALL THE VIRTUES,
BOTH FOR THEIR OWN SAKES . . .
AND FOR THE SAKE OF HAPPINESS."

—ARISTOTLE

WHAT DO the ancient fable of the Ants and the Grasshopper, the God-given right to pizza delivery, the My Lai Massacre in Vietnam, and a sex scandal involving the greatest sports star of our time have to do with happiness? Everything, really.

What if I told you that there were four key virtues that guaranteed happiness? What if I told you there are four vices that are sure to bring misery? It's true. These virtues are called the "cardinal" virtues. *Cardo* means "hinge" in Latin, and thus the door to happiness swings upon these four hinge virtues: prudence, justice, fortitude, and temperance.

If you live long enough to see your kid grow into a happy adult, you will know, without doubt, that it is in part due to the development of these virtues. There is simply no true happiness without them.

Prudence: The X-Factor

One beautiful summer day, a grasshopper was walking about singing and playing music when he came across a group of ants carrying kernels of corn to their anthill.

"Why don't you put down all that work and come play with me?" asked the grasshopper.

"We are storing food for the winter and think you should do the same," replied the ants.

"Winter is far away," said the grasshopper. "I'll do my work later. For now I will enjoy this beautiful day."

Fall came and went and winter brought freezing temperatures and a thick blanket of snow. The grasshopper could not dig through to find warmth or food and so went to the ant hill to beg for help. "Please, I am starving. Give me something to eat," he cried.

"What were you doing all summer?" asked the ants. "We were busy at work preparing for the winter."

"I did not have time," said the grasshopper. "I was too busy singing and playing my beautiful song."

The moral of the story: be prudent and know when to get to work.

*   *   *

To open the door to happiness, you must hand your child the key of prudence. Prudence has been called the "first virtue" and the "father of the virtues," but we'll give it a modern twist and call it the "X-factor." The Oxford Dictionary (believe it or not) defines the X-factor as "a special quality, especially one that is essential for success and is difficult to describe." This is exactly what prudence is in regard to the moral life. If you don't have prudence, you can't have the other virtues.* Prudence is also hard

* Some of you may be thinking that humility is the first virtue. Both prudence

to describe. It is most clearly seen in the decisions that a person makes.

Prudence is so important because it tells you what to do *and* gives you the capacity to carry it out through one of the other virtues. Aristotle says that prudence is a "true reasoned state of capacity to act with regard to things that are good or bad for man." In other words, prudence enables you to think clearly and to commit yourself to doing what is necessary to becoming truly happy.

Prudence is a thought . . . sort of. There is a big gap between a pure thought and an act, and in the middle lies the ability to commit to performing the act. This commitment is like a bridge that connects thought with one of the other virtues. Prudence takes you from thought to one of these three virtues.

Aristotle calls this bridge between thought and act "a capacity to act," which is exactly what you want your kid to develop. Teaching your kid *what* to think and *how* to think is very important, but helping him develop the "capacity to act," whether courageously or justly or temperately, is the first key to happiness.

How many times have you intended to change bad habits or take on good ones? How many times have you said to yourself, "I'm gonna lose ten pounds," or "I'm gonna stop yelling at my kids"? How many times have you resolved to pray each morning before the kids get up? We all have these good intentions, but far

---

and humility are "the first virtues" in a different sense. Prudence is the first virtue in that we must have it to acquire the other cardinal virtues. Prudence, therefore, is the foundation of the moral life. One might say prudence is the first of the "natural" virtues. Humility is the first virtue, in that we must have it to receive the theological virtues of faith, hope, and charity. Humility is the foundation of the spiritual life, i.e., our life in relation to God. Thus, one might say that humility is the first of the "supernatural" virtues. Lastly, one should note that humility is not the greatest virtue. This prize goes to charity. Humility, rather, is the first only in the sense that it is the foundation of the spiritual life.

too often we don't have the "X-factor" to make it happen. As the old saying goes, "The road to hell is paved with good intentions." Without the X-factor—without prudence—good intentions do your kid no good. Eventually, she must put her good intentions into action.

So how does a kid develop the X-factor? By doing everything we discussed in part I and part II of this book. By bringing the passions into harmony with reason. By practicing good habits, over and over and over again—maybe even for 10,000 hours like the Beatles and Bill Gates did. To develop the cardinal virtues, and in particular prudence, your kid must get his mind used to seeing the good and his emotions used to supporting, rather than distracting, his mind.

But developing prudence requires even more than harmonizing reason and the passions. Remember that your kid is not only a rational animal but also a social animal. She needs friendships of all kinds, but most important, true friendships. Prudence and the other cardinal virtues are supported by these friendships.

A good friend is a good example. Nothing affects a kid more than seeing her friend being virtuous. But beyond that, a good friend develops along with your kid. They see each other striving and failing and succeeding. They discuss these life challenges and encourage one another. Having a close friend proactively wanting you to be prudent is the surest way to become prudent. Your kids want to impress their friends. Just imagine if your kid and his friends impressed each other by making prudent decisions.

In short, your kid develops prudence—the X-factor—by being the best rational and social animal he can be. Just being human *is* the trick.

Justice and the God-Given Right to Pizza Delivery

In the mid-to-late 1990s, a fierce debate ensued over the "right" to pizza delivery.

Domino's and other pizza-delivery chains had begun *redlining*, which is the practice of refusing to offer goods or services to a certain group of people. In the case of Domino's, they refused to deliver in high-crime areas in order to protect delivery drivers. Protesters put a different spin on it. They claimed that Domino's, Pizza Hut, Avis Rent-A-Car, and other nationwide companies were not concerned with safety but were, rather, racists. The redlined areas were usually minority neighborhoods.

Domino's, for example, had developed a computer system that allowed its franchisees to flag addresses according to safety level. A green flag meant: *No problem.* A yellow flag meant: *Only deliver to the curbside. Park your car and honk your horn.* A red flag meant: *Do not enter. The area is too dangerous.* Numerous robberies and assaults led to the practice of redlining, but nothing sparked the debate like the 1994 tragic accident in San Francisco.

Twenty-two-year-old Samuel Reyes was a Domino's driver. According to David Wilcox, the owner of the franchise Reyes worked for, Reyes had just purchased a new sports car. During a delivery, someone decided he wanted Samuel's new car. A struggle ensued, and the assailant put a bullet in Samuel's chest.

Reflecting on the incident and the rationale behind redlining, Wilcox told reporters, "There are certain parts out there where the bad guys outnumber the good guys—and that worries us."

The news made headlines and sparked a passionate debate. In 1995 the Bureau of Labor ranked "driver sales worker" as one of the most deadly jobs in the United States. On the other hand, investigations uncovered that not every crime, including the murder of Samuel Reyes, actually took place in a red-flagged area. The opponents of the redlining believed it was an affront on people's constitutional rights to equal protection under the law. And San Francisco decided to take action.

In 1996 the Board of Supervisors for San Francisco approved the nation's first anti redlining law. The law made it unlawful for a business that regularly advertises home delivery to the entire city to refuse to serve any address within the city.

San Francisco decided that people have the right to pizza delivery. But does justice really demand it? Do we all have inalienable rights to "Life, Liberty, and Pizza Delivery"?

*   *   *

Before your kids can become "just," they must learn what justice is. Justice is not at the forefront of the modern mind. Parents these days don't generally sit around and think, "I hope Little Jimmy grows up to be a Just Man." But Aristotle did.

What has happened to justice? It has been hijacked by *rights*. Rights are good things, and they are good things to discuss with your kids. You want your daughter to know her rights as a woman. You want your son to know his rights as a man. The civil rights movement in America has led to a great conversion of heart for America. It is a wonderful thing that a black man can be elected president within the same lifetime of other black men who had to use a separate bathroom.

As so often is the case, however, a good thing can go too far. The rights movement has fostered complete indifference to justice in our culture. Justice is a virtue. Rights are not. Rights are things one possesses. It is better to focus on the virtue so that morality stays at the heart of our motives. During the lead-up to the 2012 presidential election, a college girl argued with Mitt Romney at a town hall meeting. She said, "So, like, you believe in freedom and stuff, right?" Romney replied, "Yes, I believe in freedom." The girl replied with anger and conviction, "Then give me free birth control!" This is not an isolated sentiment.

Many people now believe that freedom means having the *right* to *free* birth control pills. The language of rights has gone too far. As a parent, you need to direct your kid toward a notion of rights guided and defined by justice.

Justice is the habit of giving another person what he deserves. For example, my son takes out the trash every day for a small allowance. We have an agreement. If he keeps his end of the bargain, he deserves his money. It is just that I pay him. He does, in a limited sense, have a "right" to be paid if he does his job.

At times, however, we have revoked his pay as a punishment for bad behavior, like mouthing back or picking on his siblings. Even if he still takes the trash out, he can still lose his allowance. This is because he does not have a fundamental or a God-given right to an allowance. It is therefore perfectly just for me to keep the money for good reason.

On the other hand, he has a right to be loved. This is a fundamental right that I cannot revoke for any reason, nor would I ever want to. There is a stark difference between the right to be paid an allowance and the right to be loved, just as there is a difference between a right to have pizza delivered no matter where you live and the right to be treated equally under the law no matter the color of your skin.

* * *

Justice plays a unique role among the virtues because it is the only one directed at other people.

Justice is all about being a "social animal." Aristotle and the ancient Greeks cared a great deal about justice, even to the point of calling justice the greatest of virtues, precisely because it is what brings about harmony and peace within the community.

Justice is a selfless virtue that focuses on doing good for others. Our modern obsession with rights, however, has everyone screaming "ME, ME, ME!" Rights movements generally start off with noble and pure intentions but quickly turn into self-absorption. Justice, however, keeps the focus on other people.

Little kids encounter situations that call for justice every day. Think of the last time you saw your kid fight over a toy, or demand a turn on the swing. You scurry around behind her trying desperately to teach her to share.

In this little way, you are teaching your kid how to be just. Imagine if before going to the playground, you said to your daughter, "Now remember, you have a *right* to the swing. Don't let anyone tell you differently. If someone else is on it, let him know that you will not have your rights trampled on by any toddler in this town!" Of course, you wouldn't say that. Instead, you say something like, "Remember, let others have a turn on the swing. And no pitching fits!" This is justice. It's putting the focus on others, instead of giving your kid a sense of entitlement.

Your common sense as a parent helps you to focus on justice with toddlers. But as they grow up, society tells them, "IT IS YOUR SWING AND DON'T LET ANYONE TELL YOU OTHERWISE!" But this attitude does not lead to happiness. If your kid is going to open the door of happiness, justice must help bring peace and friendship with others. What sort of friendship is it when each person's sole focus is on what he gets from the other? Earlier we discussed how true friendship is more interested in loving than being loved. So is justice. A just man gives others what they deserve.

The best way to develop a sense of justice is to develop a true friendship. At an early age, your kid can learn the importance of giving to others their due. He must develop a healthy disdain for injustice. But he must also learn that merely screaming for the right to pizza delivery is beneath him.

But a sense of justice without the courage to fight for it is meaningless. Justice and courage go hand in hand, just as injustice and cowardice do.

Courage: The My Lai Massacre

On March 16, 1968, three brave soldiers flew their helicopter over the Vietnamese village of My Lai and witnessed "one of the most barbaric acts ever committed by American forces: the massacre at My Lai, in which more than five hundred Vietnamese civilians were mercilessly slaughtered." The quote is from James H. Toner, professor emeritus in military ethics at the U.S. Air War College, in his outstanding book *Morals Under the Gun: The Cardinal Virtues, Military Ethics, and American Society.*

Toner recounts how U.S. Army warrant officer Hugh Thompson, crew chief Glenn Andreotta, and door gunner Lawrence Colburn saw their own men slaughtering women, children, and the elderly. As testimony would later show, the U.S. soldiers believed the Vietcong was hiding in the village, and in the heat of passion, a bloody stain appeared on our nation's soul.

According to Toner:

> Thompson and his two enlisted men saw a teenage Vietnamese girl lying wounded in a rice paddy. Thompson popped green smoke to mark her position and radioed for help. On the ground an American soldier ran to her. Thompson expected the soldier to administer first aid; instead, to Thompson's horror, the soldier killed her. As Thompson, Andreotta, and Colburn watched the butchery of My Lai—with not a single enemy solder in sight—Thompson decided to act. He saw a group of U.S. solders chasing about ten Vietnamese who were fleeing to a makeshift bunker. Thompson set his

helicopter down in front of the advancing Americans and gave his gunner a simple, direct order. If the Americans attempted to harm the villagers, Colburn was to shoot the Americans. The group of Vietnamese was saved. As Thompson took off, he passed over a heap of bodies. Andreotta saw something move in the pile of carnage. Thompson landed, and Andreotta walked into the virtual charnel house, pulling to safety a bloodied but unhurt three-year-old boy. (Andreotta was killed in battle three weeks later.) (*Morals Under the Gun*, chap. 7)

Thompson testified against Lt. William Calley, the commanding officer in My Lai. On March 29, 1971, Calley was convicted of the premeditated murder of twenty-two civilians. He was sentenced to life imprisonment and hard labor at Fort Leavenworth maximum security prison. No other soldiers were convicted.

There was political outrage for convicting Calley, whom the public claimed had been made a scapegoat. Seventy-nine percent of Americans disagreed with the verdict. Georgia governor Jimmy Carter asked Georgians to drive for a week with their lights on as a sign of their support of Calley, and many other governors and political leaders urged President Nixon to pardon him. The White House received five thousand telegrams concerning Calley, and they favored leniency by a ratio of 100-to-1.

This political and public outrage led Nixon to reduce Calley's sentence to house arrest and to issue a limited presidential pardon. Calley was paroled from confinement by the Army and served just three and a half years under house arrest before he was released.

Thompson, on the other hand, was awarded the distinguished Flying Cross for his actions, but he refused the honor believing the Army was trying to buy his silence. The wording in the award did not make any reference to the fact that the "hostiles" who committed the My Lai massacre were Americans. Colburn has stated, "We were dishonored for telling the truth."

In 1998, however, Thompson and Colburn returned to Vietnam for a ceremony and had the privilege of meeting the young boy whom Andreotta had pulled from the pile of bodies. Toner notes that the American ambassador to Vietnam declined to participate in the ceremony because, "Neither the policy objectives of the United States nor the current relations between the U.S. and the Socialist Republic of Vietnam would be served by Embassy participation."

In the early 2000s, a few honorable voices lobbied to properly honor the men who were brave enough to stand strong against their fellow soldiers. Finally, Army leaders agreed but suggested that the ceremony be held in private to avoid bad press. Thompson wanted the award to be presented at the Vietnam Memorial in Washington D.C., but his request was at first denied. Finally, though the Army relented. A full ceremony was held at the memorial, and today the Army uses Thompson, Colburn, and Andreotta as outstanding models of courage for its soldiers.

*   *   *

If you are the parent of a little boy, you know you're the parent of a little soldier. He runs around using a wooden spoon as a gun or a stick as a sword, chasing the enemy (your dog or maybe even his sister). As he grows older, he may look to real soldiers as models of courage, as he rightly should. There are excellent models of courage in uniform. But it's vitally important that you instill in him the notion that courage is not brute strength. It is not the willingness to fight hard or risk one's life at any cost. It is not the ability to kill and avoid being killed. It's important for him to know that Thompson and his men were the courageous ones, not Calley.

What made the Christian martyrs courageous, their eyes looking toward heaven as they were thrust into the Colosseum for refusing to deny Christ? What made the shepherd boy David courageous as he faced off with the giant Goliath? For that matter, what made Thompson courageous as he stood up to his fellow countrymen?

The Christian martyrs, David, and Officer Thompson were courageous because they were willing to sacrifice themselves *for the good*. Courage is not something we do to impress another, to enrich ourselves or for the sake of some pleasure or worldly good. A thief who risks his life to steal a diamond is not courageous. He's just a thief. The kid who jumps off a bridge to impress a hot girl isn't courageous. He's just a stupid kid. A husband and father who foolishly and needlessly gives his boss a piece of his mind isn't courageous. He's just an irresponsible husband and father. Courage aims at a true good, not just a fleeting pleasure.

It is crazy for you to expect your kid to be courageous without helping him know exactly *why* he should be courageous. Every dad is a little frustrated when his kid, especially his son, is too chicken to take off the training wheels. Every dad is a little frustrated when his kid won't stay in the batter's box on the baseball field. This is understandable. But dad must ask himself precisely *why* it is good to take off the training wheels and to stay in the batter's box. If he can't articulate it, how in the world is Junior supposed to justify overcoming his fear?

In reality, Junior usually overcomes these little fears for the good of impressing dad. Kids so desperately want to impress their mom and dad that they overcome all sorts of fears. While it is a good thing to want to make mom and dad happy, there are much better reasons to do things in life. Imagine your kid saying, "Dad, I don't want to get hit by the ball. Can't we just go home?" and yourself answering, "Son, you need to impress me. Be brave, overcome your fear, and swing away." Nonsense. It's dad's job to point out the higher good for which to aim. "Son, once you get comfortable here in the batter's box, you will be able to hit the ball. And when you can hit the ball, this game becomes a lot of fun." Or "Son, you joined a team. Your team needs you to be the best you can be. So let's give it our best. The team deserves your best."

Aristotle would have mom and dad divert the attention away from the perceived good (like impressing mom and dad) and toward a greater good (like enjoying a great game or helping the team). Kids must learn at a very early age to look for the good. This is the most important step in becoming a truly courageous person.

As your kid gets older, perceived goods and actual goods get more difficult to distinguish. You've experienced this in your own life. "Am I in love with this girl, or just infatuated?" "Do I really need the new clothes, or am I justifying another spending spree?" "Have I chosen to have no more kids for the good of the family, or simply because I enjoy my own comforts?" Prudence helps guide us through such questions, but courage helps us act, even when it's hard.

Joseph Pieper says, "Only the prudent man can be brave. Fortitude [or courage] without prudence is not fortitude." At My Lai, Calley and his men completely lacked prudence. It may look brave to start shooting, but it is not. Tough guys are not necessarily virtuous guys. Thompson and his men, however, were both. They had the prudence to know what was right, and the guts to fight for it. They were willing to fire on their own men to save the lives of innocent people—a perfect example of prudence and courage coming together.

*   *   *

Earlier we talked about virtue being the mean between extremes. If courage is a virtue, what are the extremes on both ends? We've seen one extreme, as exemplified in Calley: rashness. Calley was trigger happy. But on the other end of the spectrum, you find a coward. This is someone who can't sacrifice his own comforts, his own life, for the good. Some of Calley's men knew the massacre was wrong. Apparently, they lacked the courage to stop it.

Cowardice is a big problem. Kids today are wimps, mostly because they live in the Age of Indulgence. If you give your kid a milkshake every time he pitches a fit for one; if you give your daughter your American Express card every time she wants to go to the mall; if dad has to mow the grass while junior plays inside with his Xbox on a beautiful Saturday afternoon, then of course your kids are going to grow up with an insatiable need to seek pleasure and avoid pain. Self-sacrifice is simply not in their vocabulary nor in their muscle memory.

You don't want your kid to take on discomfort for the mere sake of being uncomfortable. As Joseph Pieper wisely says, " 'Suffering for its own sake' is nonsense." Rather, you want your kid to learn that suffering can be good *if* done for a good reason. That's courage.

But as a society, we're forgetting the meaning of true courage. We don't know how to suffer for the good. It's why you see parents who can't stand up to their whiny kid. And that's why the kid develops a sense of entitlement. When something hurts, even a little, he buckles under pressure. Cowardliness, though, swings shut the door to happiness. You won't find a truly happy person who shies away from all pain and suffering. Cowardliness and happiness simply cannot go together.

Back on the other side of the spectrum of courage, we have Lieutenant Calley. He had a false sense of bravery that resulted in the deaths of defenseless women and children. In the heat of his passion, Calley must have felt like a courageous warrior. But since he lacked prudence, Aristotle would say that Calley's actions were "rash." In the case of Calley and the My Lai Massacre, we can call rashness being trigger-happy.

Therefore, the spectrum has Calley's men (the Cowards) on one end, Calley (the Trigger-Happy) on the other, and Thompson and his men (the Courageous) in the middle.

Courage without prudence is impulsive, reckless, and dangerous. As a parent, be sure to avoid courage for its own sake, for there is really no such thing. Courage must be directed toward the good, otherwise your kid can end up trigger-happy. At the same time, you don't want your kid to be a wimp, either. Your kid needs to understand that there are certain things worth fighting and suffering for.

Temperance: Staying on the Fairway

Tiger Woods was well on his way to becoming the best golfer who ever lived. He burst onto the scene as a standout at Stanford University and then took the world by storm as an amateur, winning three amateur titles in a row and consistently ranking as the highest amateur in PGA tournaments.

Woods turned pro in 1996 and won his first major, the Masters, one year later, at age twenty-two.

He was the dominant athlete of his time. He was making money hand over fist. Everyone—Gatorade, Nike, Gillette—wanted him to endorse their products. He had it made.

Woods was certainly blessed with a huge amount of talent, but his work ethic was also unparalleled. He practiced golf incessantly, from the time he was a child straight through to his time as the top golfer of the day. No matter the weather, no matter the time, no matter any other commitments, Woods put in the effort.

He was disciplined, and exceptionally so. In terms of training and athletics, Tiger Woods possessed an unmatched level of drive and temperance. And it was temperance, drive, and discipline that kept him at the top of the game for nearly fifteen years.

Then, in the early morning of November 27, 2009, that all changed. Woods crashed his Escalade into a tree and fire hydrant in his driveway and was treated for minor cuts. He called it a "private matter."

A week later a gossip magazine got its hands on a voicemail left by Woods for an alleged mistress. Woods then admitted to "transgressions." But the mess didn't stop there. In the coming days, more than a *dozen* women came forward claiming that they, too, had had affairs with Woods. Rather than denying any of the claims, Woods admitted to his infidelity and took a leave from golf.

He has since returned to the game but is nowhere near the player he once was. He and his wife have divorced. And he has lost tens of millions of dollars in endorsements after companies withdrew their support in the aftermath of his affairs.

For years—publicly at least—Tiger Woods was the picture of temperance. It was the key behind his stellar game and the basis of his lucrative endorsements. No one trained harder, had more drive, or played better than Tiger Woods. Period.

And then it all went away. A man who had built his life on temperance was destroyed by the lack of it. Not only did his career suffer, his marriage fall apart, and his endorsements disappear . . . but he also wasn't *happy*. All the women and pleasure in the world wasn't enough.

* * *

As a parent, it's your job to show your son or daughter that exercising self-control is not just a religious commandment on a couple of stone tablets. Rather, it is an essential ingredient in the recipe for happiness. It takes some work to teach your kids this, because today's culture will tell them the exact opposite.

The media show your kid that self-indulgence is the way to happiness. They've found the magic formula, and it's the same one Tony Robbins pushes. "Seeking pleasure and avoiding pain is the key to happiness!" the world screams. "For heaven's sake, you only live once. Make the most of it." And yet we know this isn't true. Tiger Woods's self-indulgence resulted in huge losses, professionally, personally, and financially. And he's just one high-profile example. The world is full of people who are casualties of the hedonistic lifestyle.

Can you think of any time of self-indulgence in your life that you regret? Maybe it's a time when you overate, got high or drunk, got in a fight, slept too much, or spent too much money on clothes. Chances are when you recall those things, you do so with regret.

Now think of those times when you skipped the dessert, saved rather than spent, turned off the TV and went to sleep, exercised, bought less than you wanted but enough for your needs, or kept your cool in the face of frustration. Chances are you don't regret those moments.

So why do you "feel good" about yourself after being temperate, and why do you "feel bad" about yourself after being intemperate? The answer lies at the heart of what the Greeks understand temperance to be.

Temperance is not about refraining from sex, drugs, and rock 'n' roll. It's much more beautiful than that. It's about an ordered self. It's about a complete and harmonious self. Temperance isn't just about grabbing the Snickers bar from your kid's chubby fingers. It's about helping him develop inner order.

Remember that your kid is an animal with passions. But your kid is different from the dogs Cesar Millan trains or the tiger that nearly killed Roy Horn. Your kid is different because she has the power of reason, which can direct her passions toward the good. At the Cheesecake Factory, we saw how most of us struggle over whether to indulge our appetites. For the strong-willed and weak-willed, there is an inner disorder. Most of your kid's life is a struggle over choosing between good and evil, but she was made for more. She was made to breakthrough to virtue, where all struggle ceases and inner harmony resides.

Temperance opens the door to happiness because it opens your soul to "serenity of spirit," as Joseph Pieper calls it. Ask yourself right now: "What do I desire for my child more than 'serenity of spirit'?" If for some reason this is not number one on your list, I bet it is very high.

To achieve "serenity of spirit" your kid must work through the inner battle between his reason and his passions. He must breakthrough to a peaceful outcome. Temperance, more than any of these virtues, provides your kid with this inner order. Temperance is more than throwing away the Dunkin' Donuts and deleting the porn on your computer. Yes, it requires bodily self-control. But it is ultimately about obtaining serenity. It is about becoming happy and content with oneself.

PRUDENCE → directed toward all of reality

JUSTICE → directed toward others

COURAGE → directed toward difficult situations

TEMPERANCE → directed inward

Temperance is the only one of the four cardinal virtues aimed at self. Turning inward, however, is a tricky thing. We often think of it as a form of relativism or selfishness. You turn inward to find truth as opposed to looking outward for it. But with temperance, you turn inward for the purpose of finding an inner peace *so that* you can share your inner peace with others. There is an old adage of the law that says, "You cannot give what you do not have."

Temperance is about developing something on the inside so you can give something to those on the outside. In this sense, you must be *selfish* so you can ultimately be *selfless*.

Your kid is naturally drawn toward selfishness because, as Joseph Pieper says, "The natural urge toward sensual enjoyment, manifested in delight in food and drink and sexual pleasure, is the *echo and mirror* of man's strongest natural forces of self-preservation" (emphasis added). Echoes bounce off everything and come at you from all directions. This is exactly what temptation is like. It is important, then, to keep your eye on the actual good from the very beginning of life's journey. That's what mom and dad are for.

True self-preservation is doing what is necessary to save the soul. Temperance turns inward to bring order to the soul for the sake of preserving it. Intemperance turns outward toward instant gratification for the sake of a perceived self-preservation. The difference is everything.

Chapter Twelve: *Playlist*

> ▸ *Cardinal* comes from the Latin word meaning "hinge." So the four cardinal virtues open and close the door to happiness.

> ▸ Prudence: The "X-factor," the "first virtue," the "father of virtues." It tells you what to do *and* gives you the capacity to carry it out through one of the other virtues.

> ▸ Justice: "I have a *right* to pizza delivery," is how used and abused the word *right* has become. A right is the flip side of justice.

Justice is giving another his due. Remember to help your kid think more about justice than "rights."

▸ Courage: Remember the *My Lai Massacre.* The cowards didn't stop Calley. The rash joined him. And the truly brave faced him down.

▸ Temperance: Remember Tiger Woods. He had incredible temperance when it came to practice and dedication to golf, but not so much when it came to women. A big amount of intemperance in one area of your life will eventually creep over to other areas.

CHAPTER THIRTEEN

Aristotle, the Beatles, and Bill Gates

"IT MAKES NO SMALL DIFFERENCE TO
BE HABITUATED THIS WAY OR THAT FROM
CHILDHOOD, BUT AN ENORMOUS DIFFERENCE,
OR RATHER *ALL* THE DIFFERENCE."

—ARISTOTLE

THE BEATLES performed for eight hours a day, seven days a week in Hamburg, Germany, when they were still a struggling high school band. Bill Gates spent countless hours programming on an ASR-33 Teletype computer in the eighth grade. Both gave it their very best and were in the right place at the right time. Malcolm Gladwell calls this the formula for becoming an Outlier. Aristotle would call it the formula for becoming happy.

In his best-selling book *Outliers*, Gladwell discusses what it takes for a person to become extremely successful. Extremely successful people don't fit into the normal spectrum of achievement. They have broken out of the box and reached a level of success in their industry about which others can only dream. They are, according to Gladwell, Outliers.

The ancient Greeks would call the success of Outliers excellence, or simply virtue. Throughout this book, we have used the word *virtue* synonymously with "moral virtue." But it is worth recalling that virtue in Greek could be applied to nearly any human achievement. We have spoken about the virtue of a musician, the virtue of an athlete, and in many other ways. If Aristotle examined Gladwell's book, as we are about to do, he would have found a lot of "virtue" in it . . . although maybe not too much moral virtue.

The 10,000-Hour Rule

The Beatles arrived in the United States in 1964. They were new to the States but not to each other: by 1964 these British kids were veterans. Lennon and McCartney started playing together in 1957, seven years prior to coming to America. As a young high school band, they had the good fortune of going to Hamburg, Germany, for some gigs. They jumped at the chance and took off. They found themselves in a small club playing through the night. It didn't pay well, it didn't get press, it wasn't even all that fun. But it was practice in front of real people.

In an interview, John Lennon explained, "In Liverpool, we'd only ever done one-hour sessions, and we just used to do our best numbers, the same ones, at every one. In Hamburg, we had to play for eight hours, so we really had to find a new way of playing." Pete Best, the Beatles' original drummer, said, "We played seven nights a week. At first, we played almost nonstop till twelve-thirty, when it closed, but as we got better the crowds stayed till two most mornings."

Gladwell does the math:

> The Beatles ended up traveling to Hamburg five times between 1960 and the end of 1962. On the first trip, they played 106 nights, five or more hours a night. On

their second trip, they played 92 times. On their third trip, they played 48 times, for a total of 172 hours on stage. The last two Hamburg gigs, in November and December of 1962, involved another 90 hours of performing. All told, they performed for 270 nights in just over a year and a half. By the time they had their first burst of success in 1964, in fact, they had performed live an estimated twelve hundred times. Do you know how extraordinary that is? Most bands today don't perform twelve hundred times in their entire careers. The Hamburg crucible is one of the things that set the Beatles apart. (*Outliers*, 49–50)

Then Gladwell turns to Bill Gates. Gates came from a well-off family in Seattle. He was a bright child and became bored at his local public school, so his parents pulled him out and placed him in an elite private school, Lakeside. When Gates was in eighth grade, Lakeside started a computer club. Lakeside was able to get cutting-edge computers that even most colleges couldn't get, including the ASR-33 Teletype, which was a terminal that had a direct link to a mainframe computer in downtown Seattle. This allowed for time-sharing, which meant the computer club had to pay for access to this link with the mainframe.

> Inspired by Dr. K. Anders Ericsson, a professor at Florida State, and Malcolm Gladwell, Dan McLaughlin has embarked on a bold mission. He quit his job and began golfing thirty hours a week. If all goes according to plan, he will log his 10,000th hour on the links late in 2016. You can track his progress and see the 10,000 Hour Rule in practice at his website: thedanplan.com

The computer club ran out of money for time-sharing very quickly. After the computer club ran out of money, the University of Washington formed a group called the Computer Center Corporation (or C-Cubed). One of the founders of C-Cubed had a son at Lakeside. This connection allowed Gates to get back to his programming. And even after C-Cubed closed down, they were in pretty tight with the computer center of the university and found a way into another group, called Information Services Inc. (ISI). At this point, Gates was getting real programming experience, something that was unique for an eighth grader in 1968.

"In one seven-month period in 1971, Gates and his cohorts ran up 1,575 hours of computer time on the ISI mainframe, which averages out to eight hours a day, seven days a week," Gladwell writes. " 'It was my obsession,' Gates says of his early high school years. 'I skipped athletics. I went up [to the university] at night. We were programming on weekends. It would be a rare week that we wouldn't get twenty or thirty hours in' " (*Outliers*, 52). "By the time Gates dropped out of Harvard after his sophomore year to try his hand at his own software company," Gladwell writes, "he'd been programming practically nonstop for seven consecutive years. He was *way* past ten thousand hours" (*Outliers*, 54–55).

As Aristotle would say, the Beatles and Bill Gates developed "virtues" in music and programming respectively. The Beatles and Gates became excellent at their trades, in part due to 10,000 hours of practice. Performing on stage became "second nature" for the Beatles. Likewise, programming became "easy" for Gates.

Gladwell's Outliers show us that it takes a long time—more than 10,000 hours!—to develop an excellence or virtue. This is true of moral virtue too. Most people suffer through imperfections, or struggle with being weak-willed. They give in to temptation easily. We suffer from overly active passions directed toward self-indulgence, but we also suffer from a weak intellect that can't control our passions. Through hard work and hours of persistence, we can move into the moral condition of being strong-willed. Here we overcome our passions and aim to do good. But we still feel the temptation. We still have the internal struggle. It hasn't become easy. We have a long way to go.

After countless more hours of hard work, after fighting through countless little battles of the will, the passions begin to turn toward desiring good. The passions learn that the most pleasant state is to unite with goodness, not to embrace a fleeting moment of pleasure. We finally become what Aristotle calls "virtuous." Choosing the good becomes easy. We are freed from moral struggle. We are far more prepared for happiness. But Aristotle also says that the hard work that brought us to this point is not quite enough.

Gladwell, too, says hard work isn't enough. In fact, Bill Gates and the Beatles' 10,000 plus hours of hard work could never have happened without external circumstances playing out just right. Neither Gladwell nor Aristotle would enjoy hearing parents tell their kid, "You can do anything you put your mind to." That simply isn't true. Your kid can do a lot, but much of his future success is, frankly, outside his hands. And this is where Aristotle's notion of friendship comes into play.

It Takes an Ancient Greek Village

Without constant access to a state-of-the-art computer when he was in eighth grade, which was highly unusual in the late 1960s, Bill Gates would still be a "highly intelligent, driven, charming person and a successful professional," says Gladwell in a 2008 interview with *USA Today*, but probably not worth fifty billion dollars. No doubt, "Lennon and McCarthy had a musical gift of the sort that comes along only once in a generation," Gladwell writes, but if they hadn't been able to cultivate this gift with the opportunity to play for 10,000 hours in a remarkably short period of time, we might never have heard of them. One of Gladwell's main points in *Outliers* is that great success is due not only to smarts and a strong work ethic, but also to opportunity.

So, too, with your kid. It takes many different external factors to help shape the person that you, or your kid, can become. In a very real way, there is no such thing as a self-made man.

Virtue is, to a great extent, developed by an individual's hard work. But happiness requires more. Aristotle explains that society and culture are equally important for leading your kid to happiness. He believed that if a little kid in Athens was going to be happy, he needed to both a) develop virtue, and b) receive the right opportunities, support, affection, and instruction from Athens. For Aristotle, there is no truly happy hermit.

In part II of this book, we discussed friendship in depth. Friendship is essential to happiness precisely because we are social creatures. Your kid needs all sorts of relationships, differing in kind and degree. Without these external factors in his life, your kid will never, ever be happy.

Do you want your kid to become an Outlier, to achieve success on the level of the Beatles or Bill Gates? Gladwell says the recipe for achieving this is 10,000-hours of practice, plus an extremely unique and supportive environment that is conducive to his fulfilling his dreams, which is more luck than anything. Gladwell would say that you can go a long way on your own effort and with the average supportive environment, but Outliers were products of far more unique circumstances. Thankfully, happiness is not so complicated.

What are the chances of becoming the next Bill Gates? What are the chances of your kid's high school band becoming the next Beatles? There is a better chance of getting struck by lighting. But aiming for happiness is far more within our control, so long as certain basic requirements are met. The analogy between Gladwell's

Outliers and Aristotle's happiness has its limits, but there is a similarity. Aristotle's recipe for happiness is very close to Gladwell's recipe for becoming an Outlier. First, happiness requires virtue, developed over long months and years of learning to curb and train the passions and strengthening the will. It also requires the support and encouragement, and the simple joy, of true friendship. Without both virtue and friendship, your kid will never reach the amount of happiness that God desires for him.

Why would Aristotle love the Beatles and Bill Gates? Because they are great examples of how your kid can obtain not just excellence in some industry, like music or computer programming, but the most important industry of all: the industry of happiness.

Chapter Thirteen: *Playlist*

- ▸ The 10,000-Hour Rule: It is required of Outliers, like the Beatles and Bill Gates, and it is required of the virtuous man.

- ▸ It takes a Greek village: Outliers also need a supportive environment to become truly excellent. This is similar to the virtuous man's needing friendship.

- ▸ Virtue + True Friendship = Happiness

CHAPTER FOURTEEN

Contemplation:
Telling Your Kid to Get Lost

"CONTEMPLATION IS THE HIGHEST
FORM OF ACTIVITY."

—ARISTOTLE

HAVE YOU ever felt like telling your kid to get lost? Aristotle gives you a great way to do so nicely.

Throughout this book, we've talked about everything from the Dog Whisperer to the Stanford Experiment. We've said that your kid is a rational animal and a social animal. But your kid was made for even more than just thinking or socializing: your kid was made for contemplation, for beholding with the intellect things good in themselves, and in fact the very highest things.

When you hear contemplation, you might think of a Christian hermit living in a cave or a Buddhist monk. This is not what Aristotle has in mind. Remember, Aristotle found excellent employment working for the emperor by training his son, Alexander the Great. Aristotle didn't live in some cave; he was in a palace. So what does he mean that your kid was made for contemplation?

Aristotle said, "Asses would prefer sweepings to gold." A donkey would much rather have a bag of oats than a sack full of money. A donkey can't do anything with money. What if you gave a bird a violin? She'd fill it with twigs and lay eggs in it. The point is that our happiness is directly related to our nature.

What, then, makes your kid happy? Aristotle studied thousands of animals and always asked himself: what makes them happy? What completes them? He saw that happiness for a particular creature was tied directly to the thing that makes that creature unique. Monkeys are uniquely good at swinging from trees, thus a jungle makes them happy. A dolphin is a remarkable swimmer, and thus would not be very happy in a three-foot pool.

So what makes your kid (and you) unique from other animals? The answer: reason. Your kid is a rational animal, and therefore he must be as rational as possible to be happy. "Happiness," Aristotle says, "is in accordance with the best thing in us." And Aristotle tells us that the best thing in man is his reason.

This sounds terrible, doesn't it? Being "as rational as possible" sounds like being a good Vulcan. Have no fear. It means far more than this. For Aristotle, this means contemplation. Contemplation is the best activity of man, which means that it is intimately linked with his rational powers. Man was made to be rational, and thus man was made to contemplate the world around him. But this does not mean sitting around doing calculus. It means much more.

The contemplative person beholds the beauty of the world, sees the truth, and appreciates goodness. He doesn't just see a good act; he sees Goodness itself. He doesn't need to "get" something out of the good act, because he has already gotten the best thing from it: a vision of Goodness itself. We Christians might call this a sacramental moment: a moment when we encounter God. This is contemplation.

Furthermore, Aristotle said that the contemplative life is very enjoyable. When you see kids playing sports or musical instruments or laughing with their friends, they are touching Absolutes and enjoying an activity for its own sake, not for mere "productivity" or "efficiency." Kids need to be kids and just enjoy being alive! This is perhaps the best definition of contemplation. Enjoy being alive!

In short, contemplation *is the process of doing things for their own sake.* God made the world to be enjoyed. Somehow, someway, Aristotle understood this. I don't know how.

Aristotle's Kid at the World Series

Aristotle is a big fan of . . . being a fan. Sport goes back to the beginning of time, but the Greeks perfected it. Playing sports and excelling at them were very important in ancient Greece. If you didn't play, you at least watched. In fact, Aristotle said watching a good game is as much contemplation as most people would ever experience.

For Greeks, sports were almost like religion. In the *Iliad* (the story of the Trojan War), Homer describes extensively the funeral sports Greek warriors played in honor of their comrades who had died. Entering the sports arena, giving it your all, pushing yourself to the limits, challenging your friends to become the best they could be—all these robust actions were ways to honor the fallen. Imagine your friend dying, then honoring him with a good boxing match!

The ancient Olympics began in 776 BC and were held until AD 394 until the Christian emperor Theodosius I suppressed them, precisely because they competed with the new state religion: Christianity. Clearly the ancients saw the contemplative—and even the spiritual—power of sport.

In the *Odyssey*, Odysseus proves his royal status as king of Ithaca by showing his great ability in throwing the javelin. He was so good that only a king would have had the time and leisure to master such a physical feat!

Aristotle believed that sport was something that exists "for itself," whereas work exists "for something else." In other words, when your kid does his chores and takes out the trash, he is doing "work," in that there is a usefulness in getting trash out of the house. He isn't taking the trash out "for the love of the home." But when your kid is outside shooting hoops until dark, he's playing "for love of the game." When your little kid runs in the yard and plays "tag," there is no hidden agenda, there is no ulterior motive such as burning calories or earning a scholarship. He just wants to run and play. This is what it means to do something "for its own sake." It's why he'd tell your kid to "get lost." There is nothing more beautiful to witness than seeing someone doing something "for its own sake."

Fr. James Schall of Georgetown University, in his essay "On the Meaning of Sport," explains how sport and contemplation are similar.

> [T]here is a certain hush, a certain absorption watching a good game, as in watching a play or listening to a concert. During the performance of such games or plays, no one hardly breathes or munches on popcorn, as Aristotle said, so enthralled is he in what passes before him.

You can easily see your kid watching the World Series on the edge of his chair—it's the ninth inning, and his favorite team is down by one as the cleanup batter steps up to the plate. This is the chance! This is the moment when something incredible can happen. This is what dreams are made of. This is the moment when a man like

Babe Ruth can point to the fence and crack one right where he said. And your kid knows it. He rises with the thrill. If his team takes the lead and wins the game, there will be screams of joy and an adrenaline rush only a fool would try to suppress.

Your kid, at this moment, is more human than he's ever been. He's stepped outside time and touched eternity. He's no longer constrained by the late night hour that made his eyes heavy in the fifth inning. He's unaware of all that's around him. He's on the edge of his seat, awaiting the miracle . . . And as the ball is pitched, your kid no longer clings to the hour, the minute, or even the second; he clings to the milliseconds that slowly tick away. He feels as if he can see the stitches on the ball despite its speed. Your kid is not just on the edge of his seat; he's on the edge of his humanity. Indeed, he has lost himself but has become the truest version of himself.

Although he cannot understand this final point, you can: it doesn't matter if his hero hits the ball. He's already lived the moment—that contemplative moment. If he gets to jump for joy, fine. If he cries in sorrow, fine. Both are more than fine—they're good.

We can only speculate whether Aristotle took his kid to the Olympics. But I can't imagine that he didn't. Aristotle would certainly advise you as a parent to take your kid to ballgames. Let your kid lose himself in watching a game. It is a very human and a very Aristotelian thing to do.

This is contemplation, albeit an imperfect version. When your kid gets lost in a game, his rational soul goes beyond the confines of his body. His mind and heart transcend his own little world. Aristotle was on to something. Just as the Christian hermit in the cave uses his prayers to move beyond this mortal world to adore God, Aristotle knew that human nature allows us to transcend our present state. He knew we were made to see more than what our eyes show us. And although watching the World Series may sound like a feeble example of contemplation, it does have its similarities to adoration of God. Worship of God is indeed the process of abandoning ourselves and embracing Him alone. Similarly, Aristotle believed that it was a good start to "go beyond" ourselves in different ways, such as sports and even music.

Aristotle's Kid at a Concert

Earlier, we noted that in today's world, you don't have to look far to find a kid with an iPod. We talked about the dangers of your kid constantly listening to his iPod, or watching TV, or playing video games. But what about when he does listen to his iPod? What sort of music should he be listening to, and how does it affect him? Aristotle puts the burden on parents to know not only how to monitor its use but to also understand the nature of music itself. This seems like a difficult job, but Aristotle makes it easy.

Has a song ever got stuck in your head? No matter what you do, you can't get it unstuck. Aristotle and the ancient Greeks understood why. Many ancient Greek philosophers argued that music is perhaps the closest thing to the human soul. Music has passion. You can hear love and hatred in music. You can hear pleasure and pain. Music can move you to sadness or joy. It can get you pumped up. It can rock you gently to sleep. Music moves the soul—there is no arguing with that.

It is no coincidence that Aristotle spoke about music in his book *Politics*, his study of society and people in society. In book 8, Aristotle writes about the education of children and the importance of different areas of study, of physical education (such as sports), and of musical training.

Music, Aristotle says, directly imitates the passions of the soul. When you listen to music, your soul is infused with the characteristics of that music. And over time, you become like that music. This is a type of transcendence . . . and it can be good or bad.

Angry-sounding music—like hard rock and gangsta rap—brings about anger in the soul. It may feel like "fun" for the moment, but over time true anger moves from the music to your soul. It is essentially like dwelling repeatedly on angry thoughts. Aristotle explains that this is because the soul is filled with passions, and it's always looking for other passions to take on. Listening to good music is contemplation. It's like a conversation between two rational people: your kid is taking in a message from the music and will respond in some way. After hearing this music, it is a part of him.

Just as angry music takes root in the soul, so too can joyful or beautiful music. A joyful melody raises the mind to good thoughts and good feelings. Don't be fooled: kids can appreciate beautiful music. And when the music takes their mind away, and you see a little foot tapping or a little head nodding with the beat, you are looking at small versions of contemplation.

Have you ever seen a great musician playing her music? She loses herself in the music just as a monk loses himself in prayer. An hour of time can feel like minutes. The soul becomes absorbed, not by selfish motives and passions, but by something beyond itself. There is a harmony, not just of musical notes, but of the musician and the music. She becomes one with her music.

Music is contemplative for the listener as well. I attended a symphony once in Salzburg, Austria, and saw some rough-looking characters come in off the street. They couldn't afford the good tickets, so they sat on the floor in the back of the great music hall. Here I was in one of the greatest music halls in the world, listening to the greatest performers in the world, and yet I couldn't take my eyes off the homeless guys sitting on the floor. They were reading along with the music in the program. You could see their eyes follow the notes on the page. During that concert, they were no longer street people; they were musicians. They were lovers of music. They became the music.

At that concert in Austria, the music had done its job. It had harmonized with the instruments, with the performers, and with the spectators. It was truly beautiful. It was at that moment that I realized that music was more than notes and chords: it is truly a spiritual activity, or as Aristotle would say, it is contemplative.

Your kid will love music. But what kind of music will you help her love? Aristotle would encourage you to help her love music that communicates the right message to her soul. It may sound simple, but keep your kid away from the junk. Keep your kid away from music that moves the soul toward aggression and hatred and anger. Lead your kid toward music that leads her soul to peace and joy. This is an excellent way to prepare your kid for the ultimate contemplation, which we address in the final chapter of this book.

Sports and music are indeed forms of contemplation. They help your kid achieve happiness, and they are important parts of your kid's life. But contemplation is more perfectly found among true friends.

Contemplation in Friendship and Marriage

There's nothing worse than a self-absorbed person. We all know one. As soon as he walks in the room, everything is about him. Every word that comes from his mouth is a search for sympathy or an effort to impress. If such a person bothers you, it's because you intuitively know that this behavior is the exact opposite of what Aristotle means by contemplation. We were made to go beyond ourselves, not get stuck on ourselves

True friendship, as we said, is all about the Other: the other person and ultimately the Ultimate Other, namely God. Just as sport takes your kid beyond himself, just as music draws his soul up into harmony with itself, so does true friendship.

Just like a kid on the edge of his seat watching the World Series, or the homeless men getting lost in the music of the great symphony, a bride and groom standing before the altar, staring into each other's eyes, are engaged in contemplation. In fact, the contemplation that occurs in marriage and in other true friendships is on an even higher plane.

Earlier we showed how true friendship leads to deep discussions between two friends about the most important things in life. This is only possible through coming together, sharing one's ideas, asking and answering questions, all in the search of truth. The process of two souls joining can't be done through tweets or texts but by coming together and engaging each other, whether in conversation or in marriage. True friendships, in the constant desire for the happiness of the other, lead to contemplation. It is truly a form of transcendence.

Your son or daughter was made for this kind of relationship. He or she was made to go beyond the self, to care more about loving than being loved, giving rather than receiving. Transcending selfish motives is perhaps the greatest form of contemplation. And true friendship is where this happens.

Marriage is ultimately where your child will unite with another in the most profound way possible for human persons. If your kid one day enjoys the vocation of marriage, it will be a vocation to transcendence beyond the self. Contemplation need not be slow and quiet, anymore than the ninth inning of the World Series is slow and quiet. You live a fast-paced life with your spouse, and yet you are called to live it in contemplation of the other (your spouse), and in that relationship to an even greater Other (God).

Think of a mother looking down at her baby, completely lost in the joy of the moment. Marriage can be this. Marriage, for your child, can be a life of contemplating the goodness of the other, the spouse, all the while leading him more and more to the contemplation of the Source of all Goodness.

Just as friendship is all about the other, so too is contemplation. Aristotle saw little versions of contemplation all around: sports, music, laughter among friends, children at play, and between husband and wife. And he understood that all these, as wonderful as they may be, are incomplete.

Chapter Fourteen: *Playlist*

- ▶ Contemplation does not mean sitting in a cave thinking about the cosmos, or sitting in the library thinking about calculus.

- ▶ Contemplation is seeing things that are good *in themselves*. It is enjoying things *in themselves*.

- ▶ Contemplation is about *enjoying life!*

- ▶ Sports, music, a good book, and good friends are all ways to "lose yourself."

- ▶ Contemplation of your spouse is one of the highest forms of contemplation. See the goodness and beauty of the *other*, not just the *good things* he or she can do for you.

— CHAPTER FIFTEEN —

Why Your Kid Exists

"EVERYTHING WE CHOOSE WE CHOOSE
FOR THE SAKE OF SOMETHING ELSE—
EXCEPT HAPPINESS."

—ARISTOTLE

In the End, Does Aristotle Let Us Down?

ALL RIGHT, I will say it. I will go ahead and give away the climax
of this book. It is this: Aristotle believed that *your kid was made to
worship God.*

This is a climax if ever there was one. It is also a bold claim,
given that Aristotle was an ancient Greek philosopher who never
benefited from divine revelation. In this final chapter, I will explain
what this means.

Despite the fact that I am a Catholic, I have tried throughout
this book not to project Christian theology onto Aristotle. It's not
an easy task. Church Fathers like St. Augustine, medieval scholars
like St. Thomas Aquinas, and countless others have relied on Plato
and Aristotle to shape Christian theology. The intent of this book,
however, has been to show how ancient philosophy applies to your

kid's life, not how early Christian or medieval theology applies to your kid's life.

But now that we are discussing Aristotle's final words on happiness, Christian thought will come to the forefront. Aristotle did as well as a pagan could without revelation. Unfortunately, he had no understanding of a personal, loving God. Pure reason brought him (and Plato) to a vague concept of divinity, but one that was completely removed from creation.

Popular Greek myths of gods entering petty fights with men and mating with their women may have led Plato and Aristotle to develop a more pure and transcendent notion of divinity in contrast. But the popular myths may also have led them to see a personal God as preposterous. An all-powerful God (unlike Apollo or Zeus) that cared about every detail of our lives was beyond Plato's and Aristotle's comprehension. But if we "baptize" Aristotle's final thoughts on happiness, that is, if we look at it with Judeo-Christian eyes, we can see it as a magnificent climax.

Before we baptize Aristotle, we should consider why Aristotle says that happiness is the ultimate end of human life. Everything that you and your kid do originates out of a desire for happiness. Everything.

Happiness in Everything

> Every art and every inquiry, and similarly every action and pursuit, is thought to aim at some good; and for this reason the good has rightly been declared to be that which all things aim.
>
> —Aristotle, *Nicomachean Ethics*

These are some of the most famous words in all history. They are the opening lines to Aristotle's *Nicomachean Ethics*. They also reveal the reason you are reading this book. We seek "the good" in everything we do because we believe good things make us happy. No matter how silly your kid may appear at times, he is always seeking happiness.

Why are you reading this book? Perhaps the cover piqued your interest. Perhaps you're planning to write a critique and dispute everything I've said. Maybe you just want to please your spouse, or maybe you're in prison and have nothing else to do. No matter the reason, you are seeking a *perceived* good that you believe will make you happy.

How are you reading this book? Are you reading it with your legs crossed? Are you reading it outside? Are you holding the book with one hand? Are you using reading glasses? All these actions are either conscious or unconscious ways of seeking happiness.

If this is true for you, it is true for your kid. Every action she takes is a pursuit of goodness. When she does her homework, she is seeking a good. When she cocks an attitude, when she is respectful, when she sneaks a cookie, when she splashes in her bubble bath or says yes to a marriage proposal . . . everything your baby girl does now and forever is an attempt to be happy. Don't forget this when she acts like an idiot.

Herein lies the problem: your kid doesn't know the difference between a *real* good and a *perceived* good. You didn't have to put the desire for happiness within her. God did that. But you *do* have to show the difference between real goods and perceived goods. Perceived goods will not necessarily lead her to happiness. Real goods will.

Before we define the difference between a real good and a perceived good, we should ask two simple questions: Why do we pursue the good in every action? Why is this desire for good so fundamental to our nature? Surprisingly, Rudy and Jerry Maguire help us find the answer.

Aristotle, Rudy Ruettiger, and Jerry Maguire

In the movie *Rudy*, Father Cavanaugh says to Rudy, "Son, in thirty-five years of religious study, I have only come up with two hard incontrovertible facts: there is a God, and I'm not him."

In *Jerry Maguire*, Jerry sees two deaf people using sign language. He learns that they signed, "You complete me." Since that time, Romeos have thought themselves romantic by using this line on their Juliets.

If Aristotle were to watch *Rudy* and *Jerry Maguire*, he would like these lines because they get to the point that humanity is incomplete. Your kid needs many things he does not have himself: food, shelter, education, friendship, and so much more. Human nature is imperfect and thus constantly striving to obtain more perfection through unity with things and other people. Your kid wants to be as perfect as possible. He will never grow tired of seeking to be more perfect. That's why you and your kid seek the good in every act, thought, and desire. But he sure does get confused about what makes him happy.

There is a God, and your kid is not him. Aristotle would like this line. Your kid needs to go beyond himself to be perfected. If we are "not God" as Father Cavanaugh said to Rudy, then we must have others to "complete" us. This is the reason your kid desires good in all she does. She wants to be completed. Happiness is completion.

The trick is figuring out which goods are real and lasting and which ones are perceived and fleeting. Otherwise our journey toward happiness will be more difficult than God intended.

Real Good vs. Perceived Good

Imagine your kid as a grown-up taking a great expedition through the desert. He gets lost. He becomes confused in the blowing sand

and blinding light. He becomes dehydrated but walks on in desperate search of an oasis. He looks off into the hazy distance and thinks he sees a pool of water. He leaps for joy and with his last bit of energy sprints toward his vision—but that is all it is. The pool of water is a mirage.

The stronger your kid's passions (in this case, thirst), the less he can distinguish between reality and perceived reality. Our passions create perceived goods, just as King David thought killing Uriah was a good idea. Our passions want to be satisfied instantly. They want to be comforted right now. They fear difficulty more than anything. And so they take the shortcut and equate perceived goods with *real* goods.

As we said in the beginning of this book, God gave your kid a built-in GPS: reason. Reason navigates us past the mirage of water and toward the living water that gives us life. As your kid overcomes small struggles and becomes strong-willed, reason begins to dictate the way. Eventually, the passions become accustomed to being led toward the *real* good, and they start craving the *real* good.

It is very difficult for a young person to see the difference between *real* goods and *perceived* goods. While his own GPS is developing, *you* must be his GPS. You do this by way of example, of course, but also by explaining how a certain temptation might seem good, but in reality is not.

Only real goods lead your kid to happiness. This is the ultimate end, which will bring this book to its own "completion."

The Ultimate End

Has your kid ever asked "Why?" over and over again?

"I have to go to work."

"Why?"

"Because it's my job."

"Why?"

"Because I have to make money."

"Why?"

The next time this begins, do what Aristotle would do; just say "Because I want to be happy." If they ask why, say it again, "Because I want to be happy." This is the rock-bottom answer. And it can save you a few minutes of torture.

Aristotle uses the example of riding a horse to show that there are many ends along the way to happiness. A person makes a bridle *so that* he can ride a horse *so that* he can take the horse into war *so that* he has a good cavalry *so that* he can win the war *so that* he can have peace for his country . . . and so on and on until he gets to happiness. Making a bridle is an end. Training a horse is an end. Winning a war is an end. Having peace is an end. But none of these are ultimate ends. The only ultimate end is happiness.

Happiness, however, doesn't just come from winning the war. Likewise, it doesn't just come from temperance or patience. It doesn't just come from friendship. Rather, happiness is a result of all these different good things coming together into harmony. As we said before, for Aristotle, virtue plus friendship equals happiness.

And so, the ultimate end—the ultimate purpose—of your kid's existence is happiness. This is what your kid desires more than anything else, no matter how he acts, no matter how he sins, no matter how he lets you down. He is desperately trying to find happiness. The path to happiness in a nutshell is this: living the virtuous life with true friends. It is simple. It is beauty. It is what your kid wants. It is what you want for your kid.

In conclusion, we will end where we began this chapter: your kid was made to worship God. This, according to Aristotle, is the greatest form of happiness.

*   *   *

As we've noted before, happiness, for Aristotle, comes from acting in accordance with "the best thing in us." And for we humans, the best thing in us is *reason*. From a Christian standpoint, we, unlike the beasts of the earth, are made in the image and likeness of God. It is our faculty of reason that allows us to have free will, to love, to forgive, and to worship God.

Your kid is a *rational* animal and therefore he must be as *rational* as possible to be happy. This doesn't mean doing calculus all day. It means contemplating all that is good and beautiful in this world, from sports to music to other people that he loves. We concluded the last chapter with a discussion of "the Other." Your spouse is not the ultimate other. God is. The highest form of contemplation according to Aristotle is contemplation of God. Your kid was made to worship God.

Aristotle doesn't say this directly. Again, he could not comprehend a personal God we could talk to, who would listen to us, and who would comfort us. But Aristotle got very close. He said that perfect happiness is the contemplation of noble and divine things. This pagan philosopher, who never read the Ten Commandments, who never heard the teachings of Moses or Christ, somehow was able to connect your kid's ultimate happiness to divinity, which we know to be the Father, the Son, and the Holy Spirit. Our God is so personal that he wants to be called "Abba," or "Daddy," and can care for all our needs. Such affection cannot be conceived without revelation.

Aristotle, however, was on to something. He says that almost everything good in life requires the presence of someone or something else. Justice requires a person to whom to be just. Courage requires an adverse situation. A successful businessman needs customers. But the philosopher—he who contemplates divine things—needs very little material comfort. He is "self-sufficient," says Aristotle, because contemplation in itself brings great peace and joy.

Aristotle did not equate contemplation with the life of a hermit. He did not want your kid to live in a cave. On the contrary, everything we have covered in this book is a prerequisite to living the "contemplative" life for Aristotle.

Part I of this book was on virtue. Part II of this book was on friendship. When you bring these together, you have happiness. As we have seen, being virtuous is active. A virtuous kid engages the world through good action. A true friend becomes more alive by living virtuously with another. There is nothing hermit-like about happiness. It is through these actions of virtue and through these friendships that humans are able to contemplate the truth, beauty, and goodness in the world, and ultimately the God who made all things.

> It is impossible for any created good to constitute man's happiness. For happiness is that perfect good which entirely satisfies one's desire; otherwise it would not be the ultimate end, if something yet remained to be desired. Now the object of the will, i.e. of man's desire, is what is universally good; just as the object of the intellect is what is universally true. Hence it is evident that nothing can satisfy man's will, except what is universally good. This is to be found, not in any creature, but in God alone, because every creature has participated goodness.
>
> —Saint Thomas Aquinas,
> *Summa Theologiae*,
> Part II/I, Question 2, Article 8

Aristotle doesn't really let us down in the end. But you must also see that he isn't enough. He knew that he didn't have all the answers for you or your kid. He is full of ancient wisdom for modern parents. He would also, however, be the first to say that it isn't too wise to disregard two thousand years of the Christian tradition. He would have given anything to have access to revelation, as we now have.

At the very end, what do we say? Well, let's start at the beginning: You have read this book because you love your kid. And you, with every fiber of your being, want to be a good mom or dad. You want to give your kid the best thing you can give.

Aristotle tells you exactly what this is at the end of the great work he wrote for his own son, Nicomachus. He says that your kid is made for contemplating God. And if we baptize him just a little, you see that contemplation is pretty darn close to worship.

Chapter Fifteen: *Playlist*

- Does Aristotle let us down in the end? Not really.

- Your kid seeks happiness in *everything* he does, no matter how stupid the behavior may look. Our desire for happiness is in our DNA. We can't help but want to be happy.

- Human nature desires happiness in every action because it knows it is incomplete.
  - ▷ *Rudy*: "There is a God and I'm not Him."
  - ▷ *Jerry Maguire*: "You complete me."

- Parents must help decipher between perceived goods and real goods.

- The ultimate end is to contemplate God directly and through all of His creation.

- Your kid was made to worship God.

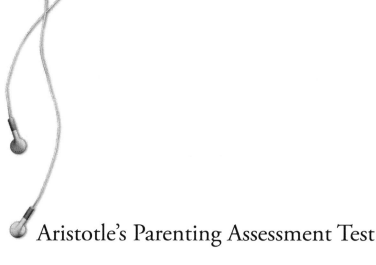

Aristotle's Parenting Assessment Test

ARISTOTLE IS the preeminent philosopher of human nature. He was a student of Plato, teacher to Alexander the Great, and one of the most influential thinkers ever to live, but Aristotle's not only for scholars. He has something important to say to everyone—especially parents.

If you want your kids to reach their full potential, you need to think about your kids the way Aristotle would. How well can you do this? If Aristotle were giving a parenting exam to modern parents, it would look something like this. See how well you score! (Don't worry. It's an open-book exam.)

1. The *most important thing* to know about your kid is his _____. Ch. 1

2. Cesar Millan is the Dog Whisperer because he understands the _____ of a dog. Ch. 1

3. The study of nonphysical reality is called _____. Ch. 2

4. Your kid's governing principle is _____. Ch. 2

5. _____ distinguishes your kid from your plant, your dog—and every other creature in the world. Ch. 2

6. C. S. Lewis and Aristotle say that your kid's emotion should not be _____. Ch. 3

7. Aristotle would call Dr. James Dobson's "strong-willed child" a "_____-willed child." Ch. 4

8. The strong-willed child and weak-willed child both _____. Ch. 4

9. The virtuous man and the vicious man do not _____. Ch. 4

10. "Doing your duty" does not *necessarily* lead to _____. Ch. 5

11. Virtue requires that your kid choose the good *for its own* _____. Ch. 5

12. Virtue is the _____ between extremes. Ch. 5

13. _____ and _____ are the extremes on either side of courage. Ch. 5

14. Friendship is the mutual recognition of _____ between two people. Ch. 7

15. A _____ judges things, actions, and people primarily upon their "utility." Ch. 7

16. The philosopher named _____ believed that pleasure was the highest good (long before Tony Robbins). Ch. 7

17. _____ percent of kid's lie on Facebook. Ch. 8

18. Aristotle says, "In poverty and other misfortunes of life, _____ are a sure refuge." Ch. 10

19. "[E]very action and pursuit is thought to aim at some _____." Ch. 10

20. The best thing you can do for your child is _____.
    Ch. 10

21. "Without friends, no one would choose to _____."
    Ch. 10

22. Children of divorce suffer more psychological problems
    than children who _____. Ch. 10

23. A _____ is the most perfect example of true
    friends coming together for the good of the other.
    Ch. 10

24. Tony Robbins's rerun philosophy is nothing more than
    "Seek _____ and avoid _____." Ch. 11

25. The Latin root word of *cardinal* means _____. Ch. 12

26. The four virtues *absolutely essential* to your kid's
    happiness are _____. Ch. 12

27. Virtue + True Friendship = _____. Ch. 13

28. _____ is the beholding of good things in themselves.
    Ch. 14

29. Three ways your kid already "contemplates" the good
    things around him include _____ and _____ and
    _____. Ch. 14

30. Every act your kid does is in pursuit of _____. Ch. 15

31. Your job is to show your kid the difference between
    _____ goods and _____ goods. Ch. 15

32. Your kid was made to _____. Ch. 15

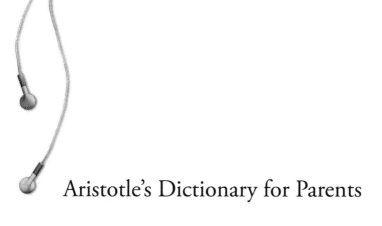

Aristotle's Dictionary for Parents

The 10,000-Hour Rule: A term coined by the best-selling author Malcolm Gladwell to explain the relentless hard work that "Outliers" must go through. It is the amount of time someone must practice his trade in order to become a true expert. The Beatles and Bill Gates are two examples. Aristotle would say that to become truly virtuous in a particular virtue, one must practice this virtue for 10,000 hours.

Apathy (*apathia*): A spiritual state in which you feel nothing. The Stoics believed this would free us from all the bad and harmful emotions we have.

Aristotle (384–322 BC): A student of Plato and tutor to Alexander the Great, one of the most influential thinkers in logic, ethics, metaphysics, politics, and the natural sciences.

Bobo Doll Experiment: An experiment in 1961 and 1963 by Albert Bandura of Stanford University that studied the influence of adult behavior on children. The experiment shows how quickly a child is influenced and mimics an adult's anger or gentleness.

Cardinal Virtues: The "hinge" (from the Latin *cardo*) virtues that open the door to happiness: prudence, justice, temperance, and virtue. They are absolutely essential for happiness.

Contemplation: The activity of comprehending the highest things that can be known, such as divine and noble things. Contemplation of good things is more fulfilling to our nature because we are "rational" beings.

Darth Vader: Sith Lord. Our example of the vicious.

Epicurus (341–270 BC): Founder of Epicureanism, which taught that pleasure was the highest good, although not hedonistic in the modern sense. It was a dignified and intellectual type of pleasure.

Friendship (in general): Friendship is the mutual recognition of well wishing between two people.

Frodo: A hobbit of the Shire. Our example of the strong-willed person.

Habit: A settled disposition to do something. Habits make things easier. We are "habitual creatures" because our nature likes to find routine. A habit is an essential component of virtue because the good act is not part of us until it becomes second nature.

Happiness: The end. The end for your kid. The reason your kid does everything he does. The culmination of virtue and friendship.

The iPod Effect: A term coined by Bernardo Carducci of Indiana University Southeast and the director of the school's Shyness Research Institute. The term is used to explain how children are getting everything instantly, from music to pizza to online movies, and thus are turning inward and become socially incompetent.

Immanuel Kant (1724–1804): a German philosopher who places duty at the forefront of moral action.

Kid's without Chests: A kid whose reason (head) or passions (gut) take control of him and who is missing the moral virtue that brings reason and passion together. C. S. Lewis came up with "Men without Chests" to show the need for people to learn to feel the right thing in the right way instead of suppressing emotion.

King David: King of Israel. Author of the Psalms. Murderer of Uriah. Our example of the weak-willed person.

Marshmallow Experiment: An experiment in 1972 by Walter Mischel of Stanford University to study "deferred gratification" and impulse control in young children. Follow-up studies on the same test subjects have been performed throughout their lives and confirm that self-control at young ages increases the likelihood of good SAT scores and overall success in life.

Metaphysics: A study of the things beyond ("meta") the physical world. The metaphysical parts of your kid include his rational powers and his eternal soul.

Milgram Experiment: An experiment in 1961 by Dr. Stanley Milgram to see if the average person would be willing to deliver a lethal electric shock to an unknown person while in the classic obedience/authority scenario.

Mother Teresa Effect: An experiment performed at Carnegie Mellon University to test whether Mother Teresa's statement "If I look at the mass, I will never act. If I look at the one, I will" applies to the average person. It demonstrates how important real (not virtual) presence is to us as social animals.

Nature: A thing's inner configuration that determines its abilities, desires, and perfection. A dog has a doggy nature and must be treated like a dog to be happy. Your kid has a human nature and must be treated like a human to be happy.

"The Other": A friend. More important, a spouse. More important, God—the Ultimate Other.

Plato: A disciple of Socrates, teacher of Aristotle, founder of the Academy in Athens. He wrote the dialogues of Socrates.

Pleasure Friendship: A mutual recognition of wishing well between two people for the sake of enjoying something together. Think of your kid's playmate next door or your golf partner. These relationships are good but limited to the pleasurable event. They are incomplete, short-lived, and too easily confused with true friendship.

Practical Knowledge: The process of learning step by step how to perform a certain function. A monkey has practical knowledge of how to open a banana. Much of our day involves this sort of knowledge and activity.

Socrates (469–399 BC): The father of philosophy, teacher of Plato, who was in turn teacher of Aristotle. Socrates was the first philosopher to place all concern on living the moral life and obtaining the afterlife, and who cared very little for this worldly life. The Oracle of Delphi called him the wisest man in the world. He concluded that he was only wise because he knew he was not. He was executed for not believing in the state gods and for "corrupting" the youth.

Speculative Knowledge: The unique ability of man to see ("speculare") the more important things in life. We use this in deep conversations with friends and family. Since our human nature was made to engage in this type of thinking, it is important for kids to do more than just text pithy comments back and forth. The speculative mind needs more than this to engage.

Stoicism: Founded by Zeno of Citium, this was a school of philosophy saying that emotions are bad and that all life should be directed by reason alone.

Rational Animal: Something that has both the passions of an animal and the power of reason.

Rational Principle: The governing entity of your kid's soul. Your kid was made to be directed by reason, not by instinct or passions alone.

Stanford Experiment: An experiment in 1971 by Dr. Phillip Zimbardo at Stanford University in which college students role-played jailers and prisoners in the basement of the Stanford Psychology building. The experiment reveals the devastating results of putting good people in a bad place.

Still Face Experiment: An experiment by Dr. Amanda Jones of Warwick Medical School for the purpose of gauging a baby's reaction to its mother's blank, emotionless face. The study reveals how social babies are, even at a remarkably young age.

Strong-Willed Person: One of the four moral characters who still desires what is evil but obeys his reason. He struggles and wins. He is not virtuous, because he still desired the evil. Frodo the Hobbit is an example.

Tarahumara Indians: A primitive tribe in the Copper Canyons of Mexico, known as the Running People, proven to be some of the best long-distance runners in the world. They are the subject of the best-selling book that has revolutionized the sport of running *Born to Run*.

Tony Robbins: A guy with big biceps, millions of crazed followers, and a two-thousand-year-old hedonistic philosophy of "seek pleasure, avoid pain."

Vicious Person: One of the four moral characters who has devolved through the weak-willed state and possesses a harmony between reason and passion as aimed at evil. He knows that what he does is evil, desires it, and feels no remorse for doing so. Darth Vadar is an example.

True Friendship: A mutual recognition of wishing well between two virtuous people for the sake of the other. Both people must be virtuous. Both care more about loving than being loved. And this is rare. You simply can't have many of these in one lifetime.

Utilitarianism: A philosophy that argues that actions are right if they are useful and beneficial to another. Utilitarians judge acts by their consequence, not by the objectivity of the act or the motive of the person acting.

Utility Friendship: A mutual recognition of wishing well between two people for the sake of being useful to each other in a particular situation. Think of your relationship with your mechanic or your kid's study partner. When the usefulness ends, the friendship ends. These relationships are good, but incomplete and short-lived.

Virtuous Person: One of the four moral characters who has worked through the strong-willed state and possesses a harmony between reason and passion. He knows what is good and desires it just the same. Socrates is a good example.

Virtue: The habit of choosing the mean between extremes in accordance with the right reasoning of a wise person.

Weak-Willed Person: One of the four moral characters who knows what is right but who succumbs to his passions. He struggles but loses. He feels remorse and tries to repent. King David is an example.

Virtue Assessment for Kids
(and for Parents too)

ARISTOTLE GAVE Alexander the Great the tools to conquer the world. With the philosopher's help, you can give your kid the tools to conquer himself. One of Aristotle's teachings is that virtue is the mean between extremes.

Assess your kid's actions and passions as Aristotle would: does he have too much of a good thing, not enough, or just the right amount? Check the box that applies for each of your kid's actions and feelings below.

What Your Kid Does and Feels	Too Much	Just Enough	Needs More
Anger	☐ Hot Head	☐ Even-Keeled	☐ Apathetic
Pleasure	☐ Self-indulgent	☐ Temperate	☐ Vulcan
Self-Esteem	☐ Big Head	☐ Confident	☐ Eeyore
Spends Money	☐ Wasteful	☐ Generous	☐ Scrooge
Fear	☐ Wimp	☐ Brave	☐ Rash
Affection	☐ Clingy	☐ Affectionate	☐ Prude
Humor	☐ Buffoon	☐ Funny	☐ Wet Blanket
Expressiveness	☐ Braggart	☐ Humble	☐ Fake Humility
Social Ability	☐ Social Butterfly	☐ Friendly	☐ Nerd
Manners	☐ Butt Kisser	☐ Polite	☐ Brat

Did your kid pass Aristotle's test?

If your kid is on either extreme, you have work to do. Turn the page for help getting him or her back to the mean.

Aristotle in Action

— Temperance —

THE ISSUE: Homework Skipping

Your kid has discovered the joy of watching sports—a good activity and even a form of contemplation. Aristotle would approve. The problem: There's an engrossing game on ESPN every night, and your kid is staying glued to the tube rather than sitting at his desk getting his homework done.

THE SOLUTION:

Teach your kid how to moderate his passion for watching every NFL or NBA game.

AVOID THE EXTREMES:

Don't be overly restrictive. Telling your kid, "No more football games, ever!" is counterproductive, and fails to recognize that your kid's desire, in moderation, is a good thing.

Don't be too easy-going. Letting your kid watch as much football as he likes is a recipe for producing a weak-willed couch potato who will be living in your basement until he's fifty-seven years old.

ACHIEVE THE MEAN:

Allow your kid a reasonable amount of time for sports watching . . . after he gets his homework done, and his chores. Make sure he maintains a balance in his leisure activities—playing outside, reading, cultivating friendships, as well as watching sports.

Remember, developing the good habit of temperance takes time.

TIP TO REMEMBER: Practice Makes Perfect:

Your kid probably won't find giving up his excessive sports-watching easy, at least at first. By obeying your reasonable rules limiting his TV time, he'll be developing his moderation muscles, and training for the day when temperance is easy.

OR point to a mentor. Inspire your kid in developing the virtue of temperance by pointing to an attractive mentor who embodies the virtue in his or her own life. "You like sports as much as your Uncle Joe. He's a great Red Sox fan his whole life and loved to watch their games on TV as a kid. But he had to miss a lot too, since school, work, and family always came first. That's why he's been so successful . . . and able to buy his box seats!"

— Courage —

THE ISSUE: Standing up to the school-yard bully

Your kid has become the target of a punk kid at school. It takes a while for you figure it out, but its been happening for a while. Your kid didn't say anything out of embarrassment. You've had it, but you're not sure how to advise your kid.

THE SOLUTION:

Help your kid learn develop the ability to confront difficult situations despite his or her fear.

AVOID THE EXTREMES:

Avoid being a hot-head. Don't encourage anger or violence. Telling your kid, "Never take crap from anyone. Teach him who's boss. Aim for jaw!", is counterproductive. This is equivalent to saying "Listen to your passions each and every time." This is dangerous advice.

Avoid being a coward. Your kid needs the confidence to stand up for himself. Tucking his tail, constantly ducking around the nearest corner in the hall, and hiding bumps and bruises from Mom and Dad is not OK. In fact, bullies are looking for easy prey that will just lay down and play dead, never willing to display confidence and strength.

ACHIEVE THE MEAN:

Tell your kid that bullies are looking for scaredy cats; they are easy targets. But at the same time, a bully might find a need to prove how tough he really is when confronted by a hot-head. Show your kid that taking the middle way will not only help them with bullies, but it will help them along the path to courage as well. Show the bully, through words, body language, or even by informing a teacher, that you are not afraid of him, and yet, you are not anxious to get into bloody fight either. Ninety-nine percent of the time, this defeats the bully without ever using your hands.

Remember, developing the good habit of courage takes time.

TIP TO REMEMBER: Courage is mental, physical, and spiritual:

1) Mental: your kid must understand the extremes. Talking it through and getting him to explain the extremes in his own language is most productive. Get your kid's head straight, first and foremost.

2) Physical: courage comes easier to kids that are physically active because they have faced difficulty, pain, and opponents. This is yet another reason for sports. If you kid isn't athletic, fine, but he or she needs to actively engage the body with exercise and outdoor activity. This will help your kid feel empowered rather than a wimpy computer geek.

3) Spiritual: your kid can learn at a very early age to look for the moral high ground in every situation. He or she must know that they are not merely a brain and a body, but they are also a spiritual being that must live according to moral virtue. Yes—it is possible for your kid to think, "I can be mentally tough, physically tough, and spiritually tough . . . all at the same time!"

OR point to a mentor. Find a relative or friend who has great self-confidence. Avoid arrogant people; kids perceive arrogance as fast as adults. If you can't think of someone you know with great confidence, think of a character in a book or movie that your kid would know. Heck, even Super Heroes can do the trick. Show your kid how these truly courageous people never look for a fight, but also protect themselves . . . and others.

— Justice —

THE ISSUE: Younger brother breaks older brother's LEGO set

Your ten-year-old has worked long and hard on building a 500 piece LEGO set. The six-year-old begged to help, but "No way" was the answer. Six year old picks up a pillow and throws it at the half-built masterpiece, shattering it to pieces. Older brother is about to explode with anger and revenge. He starts looking for something belonging to the six year old, so he can break it . . .

THE SOLUTION:

Teach your kid to enact real justice, not revenge.

AVOID THE EXTREMES:

Don't expect the ten-year-old to be a martyr. Telling your kid to "Suck it up. That's what happens in a family," will only make him think you don't care about him and that therefore he must stick up for himself—taking justice "into his own hands."

Don't give your kid free reign to make himself feel better. Letting your kid react out of revenge only makes a bad habit. Curb the emotional response immediately, before everyone is in tears screaming, "I hate you!"

ACHIEVE THE MEAN:

Let your kid see that you will help him bring about justice. Assure him that the six year old was wrong, that he will be punished, and that you are very sorry this happened. Let the ten year old feel supported, defended, but also kept in his proper place as well. "I not only will help you protect your LEGOs, but I will also help you protect your soul." Yes, a ten-year-old really can grasp this.

TIP TO REMEMBER:

Socrates said, "It is better to suffer injustice than to commit it." Your ten year old needs to understand (and he can) that taking revenge on the six year old truly hurts himself more than his brother. But if he seeks true justice, he helps his brother and himself at the same time.

Notes

If Aristotle's Kid Had an iPod is in large part a moden adaptation of Artistotle's *Nicomachean Ethics*. The *Ethics*, which Aristotle wrote as a guide to happiness for his son Nicomachus, is history's best parenting book. I am indebted to it—and informed by it—on every page.

The truth of Aristotle's insights are acknowledged by saints and scholars, illustrated in literature and popular culture, even empirically demonstrated by modern science. In the notes below, I give more information on the scholars, stories, and studies I referenced that support Aristotle. I hope you find them as fascinating as I have.

Introduction

Who is Aristotle?: The best summary of Aristotle's life and works (and furthermore, one of the best collections of philosophy ever done) is by Frederick Copleston, S.J., in his *A History of Philosophy: Volume I: Greece and Rome. From the Pre-Socratics to Plotinus*, (New York: Doubleday 1962).

A concise biography of Aristotle's philosophy, his influence, and life is found in Richard McKeon's introduction to *The Basic Works of Aristotle*, ed. Richard McKeon (New York: Random House,

1941). This is the primary text that I use for all Aristotle's works. There are more modern translations available, but those published in this collection are reliable, widely read and cited, and what I began with years ago.

PART I: VIRTUE

Chapter One: Aristotle and the Dog Whisperer

The Dog Whisperer: I've been a big fan of Cesar Millan since his show began. I'm also a big fan of Malcolm Gladwell, not only a best-selling author but also a real philosopher who skillfully uses case studies, statistics, and everyday observations to illustrate a deep truth about human nature. Gladwell uses the Dog Whisperer in his book *What the Dog Saw: And Other Adventures* (New York: Hachette Book Group, 2009). His chapter by the same name featured the story of Lori and Bandit and was the perfect example of my point: a good dog owner must understand the nature of a dog, and good parent must understand the nature of a kid.

Although I didn't dwell on it in the chapter, Lori is more than just a foolish dog owner; she is a foolish parent who didn't seem to care for her own child as much as she did for Bandit.

Seigfried and Roy: The Discovery Channel has created a digital reenactment of the tiger act based on the eyewitness accounts. You can find this on YouTube at http://www.youtube.com/watch?v=1HHPo3qxomQ

Chapter Two: A Rational Animal

Babies doing math: Dr. Karen Wynn's studies was nicely summarized by the *New York Times* here: http://www.nytimes.com/1992/08/27/us/study-finds-babies-at-5-months-grasp-simple-mathematics.html?pagewanted=all&src=pm.

The reader should not construe my inclusion of this experiment as "proof" that we are uniquely rational animals. Many animals can do basic in a manner similar to these five-month-old babies. The point, however, is simply that parents can detect one aspect of the rational faculty developing at a very young age. Monkeys use basic reasoning skills to peel a banana but never go much further than that. Only in humans does the rational faculty have the potential to lead to contemplation, as discussed later in the book.

Liberals aren't reproducing themselves: "If your parents don't have children, you won't either." Philip Longman's article on the "Liberal Baby Bust" is here: http://www.usatoday.com/news/opinion/editorials/2006-03-13-babybust_x.htm. His personal page is here: http://newamerica.net/user/92. There are some great YouTube videos of Longman also. The most important one I have found is of an event that occurred in Moscow on June 29, 2011 in which Longman addressed the Moscow Demographic Summit about the problems with infertility and the failure of nations to replace themselves. The video can be found here http://www.youtube.com/watch?v=tUnzZBupDr0. Longman presented to the summit images of the traditional "Family Tree" and how elderly people throughout history have had numerous relatives to care for them in old age. It is not uncommon now, however, for a person to have *literally no direct relative on earth*. His graphs show the typical mid-twenty-first-century family tree of one-child families, resulting in no siblings, no aunts and uncles, no cousins, no nephews nor nieces. The result is that entire family lines are becoming extinct. The "forces of mortality," he says in this lecture, are out running the "forces of fertility?" He asks the question, "Will the human race become extinct?"

Chapter Three: Kids without Chests

C. S. Lewis's chapter entitled "Men without Chests" is from his book *The Abolition of Man* (New York: McMillan, 1944).

The story of Stevie Walker, narrated by William Shatner, is found here: http://www.youtube.com/watch?v=m5Ff89mLXfU.

Chapter Four: The Four Moral Characters

King David and Bathsheba: The story is found in 2 Samuel 11. My narrative left out the happy ending. In David's old age, Bathsheba secured the succession of the throne for her son Solomon instead of David's oldest son Andonijah (cf. 1 Kings 1:11–31). God offered to give King Solomon anything he wanted. Solomon asked only for the ability to judge God's people with an understanding heart and to discern between good and evil. He has therefore been known as the wisest man to ever live.

Here we can see a similarity between Solomon and Socrates. They both desired wisdom more than any treasure on earth. But more important, they were both humble enough to know a) wisdom is what they needed, and b) they did not have enough of it.

The Marshmallow Experiment: The *New Yorker* made this study famous. There are numerous videos on YouTube, all of which are hilarious, showing the experiment in action. Watch a few with your spouse and try it with your own kids!

The Lord of the Rings is in the top six most-popular films of all time worldwide: Most people aren't aware that J. R. R. Tolkien's *Lord of the Rings* is not simply a cool kid's story and entertaining movie trilogy; it is one of the greatest works of literature in all history. It is right up there with Homer, Virgil, and Dante. No joke. Future generations, including your own great-grandchildren, will study this in literature courses in the finest universities of the day. Many readers have praised *The Lord of the Rings* as the best literary work of the twentieth century. C. S. Lewis agreed.

Chapter Five: If It Ain't Easy, It Ain't Virtue

Interview with *Born to Run* author: Author Christopher McDougall's interview can be found on the Amazon page for the book: http://www.amazon.com/Born-Run-Hidden-Superathletes-Greatest/dp/0307266303. There is also a good video at this same link.

The pros and cons of Kant: Someone once joked that Immanuel Kant "kant get anything right." Although this is a nice play on words, I think it is wrong.

There are countless resources on Immanuel Kant online, but you have to be very careful what you read. A good overview is that of Frederick Copleston, S.J., in his *A History of Philosophy: Volume VI: From the French Enlightenment to Kant* (New York: Doubleday 1964). See chapter 14 on Kant's morality and religion.

In this book I didn't get into Kant's famous *categorical imperative*, which is basically the belief that you should only act if you think all people should act the same way. Think of it more like a "universal law." This is the driving force behind his "duty" ethics. This sounds fine, but Aristotle is the better and richer philosopher because his ethics are rooted in the more foundational good of achieving happiness, rather than simply fulfilling duty.

Here are some of the key distinctions between Kant and Aristotle:

1. For Kant, reason and passion are always in conflict; for Aristotle, reason can direct the passions and become harmonious with them (in "the chest," as C. S. Lewis says).
2. For Kant, therefore, there is only strong-willed and weak-willed;

Aristotle also has virtuous and vicious.

3. For Kant, duty is the whole kit and caboodle; for Aristotle, happiness is the whole kit and caboodle.

Kant, however, has his strengths. I admire a philosopher who thinks through an entire system without being constrained by previous ones. Kant did this. His understanding of what it means to be "rational" is excellent. He drew strong and tempting distinctions between our knowledge through sense perception (a receptive / passive knowledge) and our metaphysical knowledge (an active knowledge derived from "pure logic"). He took "duty" as far as it can go, trying to develop a moral code all people could follow. And frankly, I think it is helpful to ask yourself in accordance with his categorical imperative, "Should it be a universal law that all people do what I am considering?" I personally call this the "*New York Times* Test": would I do XYZ if I knew it was going to be on the cover of the *New York Times* tomorrow morning?

Saint Augustine: In his commentary on 1 John 4:4–12, Augustine wrote famously "Love, and do what you will." This is very Aristotelian. If you love what is lovable, then you will only do good things. If you "love" an evil, it isn't truly love, so it is wrong to do it. In a sense, then, you can tell your kids, "You can do anything you *truly* want!" because, at the deepest level, they desire only things that are good. It is their flawed nature that confuses them. But I DO NOT recommend using this as a pedagogical method.

Augustine's full quote can be found here: http://www.newadvent.org/fathers/170207.htm.

PART II: FRIENDSHIP

Chapter Six: Your Kid Is a Social Animal

Could you be a Nazi? Your knee-jerk reaction is, "Of course not!" Most decent people would say the same. But our social nature makes us gravely susceptible to evil influence, as well as capable of deep friendship. It is nice to think we could never be a Nazi. But this reassuring thought is the very thing that *will lead* a person to become one. The best hedge against an evil influence is to a) know of its existence, and b) know your susceptibility. This humility, this recognition, will keep you and your kid far safer than a sense of superiority and self-righteousness.

Milgram's Experiment: There are a few different modern versions of this experiment. It is shocking to say the least! It is amazing to see real, living people willing to deliver a lethal shock to a complete stranger. Go to YouTube for videos of this experiment.

The original report of the results of Milgram's study can be found in the *Journal of Abnormal and Social Psychology* 67 no. 4, (Oct 1963): 371–8.

The Stanford Experiment: The director of this experiment, Philip Zimbardo, is still very active in related psychological studies. There are two websites worth noting. First is www.prisonexp.org, run by Dr. Zimbardo. It provides all the information you want on the experiment. It has videos of the real footage, slideshows explaining what is happening in still pictures, and even present-day commentaries from participants in the experiment. There are discussion questions, such as the following:

- If you had been made a guard, what type of guard would you have become? How sure are you?
- What is identity? Is there a core to your self-identity independent of how others define you? How difficult would it be to

remake any given person into someone with a new identity?

- Do you think that kids from an urban working-class environment would have broken down emotionally in the same way as did our middle-class prisoners? Why? What about women?
- After the study, how do you think the prisoners and guards felt when they saw each other in the same civilian clothes again and saw their prison restored to a basement laboratory hallway?
- Was it ethical to do this study? Was it right to trade the suffering experienced by participants for the knowledge gained by the research? (The experimenters did not take this issue lightly, although the slide show may sound somewhat matter-of-fact about the events and experiences that occurred.)

The second website is Dr. Zimbardo's personal website: http://zimbardo.socialpsychology.org. It covers the many other topics that Dr. Zimbardo is currently researching and provides summaries of his books, such as the *Lucifer Effect: Understanding How Good People Turn Evil*. See www.lucifereffect.com.

The Still Face Experiment: This experiment has also been performed many times. A good example by Dr. Edward Tronick, director of the Child Development Unit at Harvard University, and can be found on YouTube.

The Bobo Doll Experiment: The problem with Albert Bandura's 1961 experiment is the objective: to prove that all behavior is learned through social interaction rather than inherited traits. The findings are still heavily debated, as shown at a very interesting website: www.experiment-resources.com. The link directly to the Bobo Doll page is here: http://www.experiment-resources.com/bobo-doll-experiment.html. Videos are included from the original experiment.

Chapter Seven: The Three Types of Friendship

Overview of friendship: A great book for young parents and even older teenagers is by a friend of mine, Dr. John Cuddeback. His book *True Friendship: Where Virtue Becomes Happiness* is available from Epic Publishing. He's also given an outstanding four-hour course on true friendship for Catholic Courses, (www.catholiccourses.com), for which I was proud to serve as executive producer. John's course is filled with helpful visual aids, making it entertaining and informative. If you have teenagers, it is worth watching together.

Utilitarianism: This philosophy is a bigger problem than you may think. The most famous of modern utilitarians is John Stuart Mills. Utilitarianism is sneaky. Each part of it sounds good, but then at some point you realize, "Oops! How did I get here?"

Mills and other utilitarians believe that happiness is the end. Sounds good. But it is the end *not* for an individual but for as many people as possible. What happens, then, is the individual becomes a means to a "greater" end. The twentieth century saw the devastating effects of this philosophy at work.

Chapter Eight: If Aristotle's Kid Was on Facebook

Stats on the dangers of the Internet: Fascinating stats can be found at: www.pewinternet.org on all sorts of topics regarding your kid and the Internet.

The Mother Teresa Effect: The Heath brothers have helped make the Mother Teresa Effect popular. If you liked this book, you'll love *Made to Stick: Why Some Ideas Survive and Other Die* (New York: Random House, 2007) and *Switch: How to Change Things When Change Is Hard* (New York: Broadway Books, 2010). They can help you make certain ideas "Stick" with your kids and "Switch" their behavior. Great reads.

People were made to eat dinner together. The quote distinguishing humans from the animals eating at a trough is from *Ethics*, bk. 9.9. This entire section helps explain why humans use the dinner table for important engagements: a romantic dinner, a business dinner, friends gathering at the pub, and important international affairs. Basicallyn every important human encounter potentially involves food. This is not because we humans must eat every so many hours to stay alive. It is because *food spurs on conversation.* Perhaps it is simply because we are forced to open our mouths when eating. More likely, it is because eating is an intimate thing. You don't eat with strangers. Eating is reserved for friendly encounters.

Earlier in this same section of the *Ethics*, Aristotle talks about how a virtuous person enjoys good things *in themselves*. Bad men enjoy distorted, corrupt versions of good things. But a good man is able to see past a thing's utility or how it supports his greed or pride or lust. He sees the goodness or beauty of a thing or person in itself. And therefore, he enjoys it on a much deeper level than a bad man does.

It is for these reasons, says Aristotle, that a virtuous man enjoys life. "And life is among the things that are good and pleasant in themselves, since it is determinate and the determinate is of the nature of the good; and that which is good by nature is also good for the virtuous man."

He concludes this section with explaining that if a virtuous man enjoys his own life, then he will enjoy the life of other virtuous man, particularly his friends. And therefore, "The man who is to be happy will therefore need virtuous friends."

Chapter Nine: If Aristotle's Kid Had an iPod

Your kid and the media: For more Nielsen stats and figures on how much time the average kid spends online, plugged into his

iPod, in front of the TV, and on the phone, go here: http://www.
mediapost.com/publications/article/152661/

The iPod Effect: For more on "the iPod Effect" and the work of
Bernardo Carducci.

Visit the website for Carducci's Shyness Research Institute. You
can even participate in his studies—http://www.ius.edu/shyness/

The Dangerous Book for Boys: If you haven't heard of this book,
check it out and buy it right away.

The authors, Conn and Hal Iggulden, provide a how-to guide
for virtually every cool outside activity a kid can do, from making
a bow and arrow, to building a fort, to skipping stones, to tracking
animals, to building a campfire.

Chapter Ten: The Other: From the Sandbox to the Altar

Modern man is losing friends: The 2006 study in the *American
Sociological Review* is titled *Social Isolation in America: Changes in
Core Discussion Networks over Two Decades*, by Miller McPherson,
Lynn Smith-Lovin, and Matthew E. Brashears. The online version
of this article can be found either here: http://asr.sagepub.com/
content/71/3/353, or through Duke University's website (for the
Blue Devil fans): http://sites.duke.edu/theatrst130s02s2011mg3/
files/2011/05/McPherson-et-al-Soc-Isolation-2006.pdf.

This article shows in stark detail how friendship today is in
serious decline. Aristotle would say it is precisely because all technology and frantic lifestyles are isolating. Human nature is not
made for isolation. Aristotle said that without friends, no one
would choose to live.

The key takeaway from the study: The average number of confidants we have today has fallen almost 30 percent in twenty years,
from 2.95 to 2.08.

The study also shows an interesting change since 1985. More

people rely on their spouse as a confidant(e). This sounds good, but given the context, I don't think it is. People have a natural desire to speak with others on personal matters. The same table shows that ALL other types of relationships have declined significantly, and so a person has to "dump" everything on his or her spouse. Men and women need outlets other than their spouse.

How divorce affects children: The statistics from Dr. Robert Emery can be found on his personal website, www.emeryondivorce.com.

PART III: HAPPINESS

Chapter Eleven: The Real Role of Pleasure

Lord of the Rings: For more great resources on *The Lord of the Rings*, I recommend the following two products:

1. The Catholic Courses video or audio course by Joseph Pearce at www.catholiccourses.com, (again which I executive produced). My Catholic Courses team provides countless visual aids to keep the subject engaging. This course is appropriate for the whole family. You will greatly enjoy it, particularly if you watch it with your kid.
2. *J.R.R. Tolkien's Sanctifying Myth: Understanding Middle-Earth,* by my friend Bradley Birzer.

The Ring of Gyges: Glaucon and Plato's discussion of the Ring of Gyges can be found in book 2 of the *Republic*, available to read here: http://www.gutenberg.org/files/1497/1497-h/1497-h.htm.

Chapter Twelve: The Cardinal Virtues: Opening and Closing the Door to Happiness

Overview: A great summary of the influence and significance of the cardinal virtues in the history of philosophy, theology, and your personal life is found at New Advent: http://www.newadvent.org/cathen/03343a.htm.

Another great resource on how the cardinal virtues directly affect your happiness is *Introducing Moral Theology: True Happiness and the Virtues*, by William C. Mattison III (Michigan: Brazos Press, 2008).

The God-given right to pizza delivery: For an early newspaper article on the debate on redlining, with the headline "Pizza shops are accused of racism," see http://news.google.com/newspapers?nid=2519&dat=19960712&id=PCpdAAAAIBAJ&sjid=5IoNAAAAIBAJ&pg=1838,1602830. This article references the death of twenty-two year old pizza delivery man Samuel Reyes.

My Lai Massacre and other military case studies: See James H. Toner's outstanding book *Morals under the Gun: The Cardinal Virtues, Military Ethics, and American Society.*

Dr. Toner is the nation's premier expert on military ethics and just war theory. This book provides case studies for each of the cardinal virtues. He also emphasizes how the military, with all its faults, is still and always should be the role model of ethics in society. The virtues are most manifested in life-and-death situations, and so it is essential that the military keep the virtues at the heart of all it does.

Chapter Thirteen: Aristotle, the Beatles, and Bill Gates

Outliers and the 10,000-Hour Rule: Gladwell's book *Outliers: The Story of Success* is a great read, and once again Gladwell shows himself to be a real philosopher as well as a masterful writer. The 10,000-Hour Rule made famous by Gladwell is not perfectly analogous to Aristotle's process of developing virtue, but it's close. There is no shortcut to virtue, just as there is no shortcut to becoming an outlier. Long hours of hard work are necessary. But there is always a light at the end of the tunnel. Things get easier as we become better at them.

Additionally, the Outlier's supportive environment is not a perfect analogy to Aristotle's friendship, but it is similar. Both provide the external circumstances necessary to excel.

Chapter Fourteen: Contemplation: Telling Your Kid to Get Lost

Leisure: The leading book on the importance of "leisure," is *Leisure: The Basis of Culture*, by Josef Pieper. It is one of the best books of the 20th Century. A free download is here: http://archive.org/details/leisurethebasiso007390mbp.

It is very important for a parent to see the difference between laziness and leisure and this book will explain that difference.

Sports as contemplation: James V. Schall of Georgetown has written extensively on the subject in two short books, *Play On: From Games to Celebrations*, and *Far Too Easily Pleased: A Theory of Play, Contemplation, and Festivity*. Everything written by Schall is truly outstanding. He is one of the greatest minds of the past fifty years.

Marriage and "the Other": Archbishop Fulton Sheen wrote a wonderful book titled *Three To Get Married*. It is available through Scepter Publishers at www.scepterpublishers.com.

Chapter Fifteen: Why Your Kid Exists

Happiness in general: For an excellent overview of happiness and the influence of Aristotle's notion of happiness on the Catholic intellectual tradition, see New Advent at http://www.newadvent. org/cathen/07131b.htm.

Acknowledgements

Who reads an acknowledgments section of a book, other than those who write it? Probably no one. They sound like those silly people receiving an Oscar, rattling off names that no one knows, calling everyone they work with "brilliant." So I'll try to make this more interesting.

I would like to first thank the really bad parents I have encountered. Your tyrannical children have given me great material.

And I would like to thank the really bad parenting books I have tried to read but couldn't. You put the fire in my belly to write something for normal people.

All kidding aside, there are those to whom I send my deepest appreciation.

First, to the late Fr. John Bradley, who was the first professional philosopher I ever knew. How I wish you were here these days.

To my professors in school, particularly Dr. John White and Monsignor Sokolowski. You inspired me every day I sat in your class. And because of you guys, I could never get this stuff out of my head.

To my editors, Christian Tappe and Rick Rotondi. I couldn't have asked for better teammates. And this book *was definitely* teamwork. Your handiwork, patience, and support will never be forgotten. Many thanks to Caroline Kiser and Chris Pelicano for their excellent design work.

To my parents, who both taught me through word and action the principles in this book and provided me the opportunities to learn them. Thank you, and I love you.

Finally, to my wife. After eighty-thousand-plus words (and thirty thousand deletions), I am speechless. I love you more than yesterday and less than tomorrow.

And to Aristotle, for coming up with all this stuff. Great job!

✠ SAINT BENEDICT ✠ PRESS

Saint Benedict Press, founded in 2006, is the parent company for a variety of imprints including TAN Books, Catholic Courses, Benedict Bibles, Benedict Books, and Labora Books. The company's name pays homage to the guiding influence of the Rule of Saint Benedict and the Benedictine monks of Belmont Abbey, North Carolina, just a short distance from the company's headquarters in Charlotte, NC.

Saint Benedict Press is now a multi-media company. Its mission is to publish and distribute products reflective of the Catholic intellectual tradition and to present these products in an attractive and accessible manner.

 TAN · BOOKS

TAN Books was founded in 1967, in response to the rapid decline of faith and morals in society and the Church. Since its founding, TAN Books has been committed to the preservation and promotion of the spiritual, theological and liturgical traditions of the Catholic Church. In 2008, TAN Books was acquired by Saint Benedict Press. Since then, TAN has experienced positive growth and diversification while fulfilling its mission to a new generation of readers.

TAN Books publishes over 500 titles on Thomistic theology, traditional devotions, Church doctrine, history, lives of the saints, educational resources, and booklets.

For a free catalog from Saint Benedict Press
or TAN Books, visit us online at
saintbenedictpress.com • tanbooks.com
or call us toll-free at
(800) 437-5876